Essential
Maui

by
GEORGE KEAN

George Kean lives and works in Spain. He is the author of four Spanish titles in the current series of *Essential* guides.

AA

Produced by AA Publishing

Written by George Kean
Additional research by Jens Poulsen
Peace and Quiet section
by Paul Sterry
Series Adviser: Ingrid Morgan
Copy Editor: Edwina Johnson

Edited, designed and produced
by AA Publishing. Maps ©
The Automobile Association 1993.

Distributed in the United Kingdom
by AA Publishing, Fanum House,
Basingstoke, Hampshire,
RG21 2EA.

The contents of this publication
are believed correct at the time of
printing. Nevertheless, the
publishers cannot accept
responsibility for errors or
omissions, nor for changes
in details given. Assessments of
attractions, hotels, restaurants and
so forth are based upon the
authors' own experience and,
therefore, descriptions given in
this guide necessarily contain an
element of subjective opinion
which may not reflect the
publisher's opinion or dictate a
reader's own experience on
another occasion.
**We have tried to ensure
accuracy in this guide, but
things do change and we would
be grateful if readers would
advise us of any inaccuracies
they may encounter.**

A CIP catalogue record for this
book is available from the British
Library.

ISBN 0 7495 0515 X

Published by The Automobile
Association.

This book was produced using
QuarkXPress™, Aldus
Freehand™ and Microsoft
Word™ on Apple Macintosh™
computers.

Colour separation by BTB
Colour Reproduction Ltd,
Whitchurch, Hampshire

Printed by Printers Trento S.R.L.,
Italy

Front cover picture: Royal Palace

Contents

This book employs a simple rating system to help choose which places to visit:

 top ten

 do not miss
◆◆ see if you can
◆ worth seeing if you have time

Introduction and Background

INTRODUCTION

Spain celebrated many events of universal interest during 1992: the Quincentenary of Cristóbal Colón's (Christoper Columbus's) arrival in the Americas; the six-month-long extravaganza of EXPO '92 in Sevilla (Seville); the Summer Olympic Games in Barcelona; and Madrid's nomination as the 1992 Cultural Capital of Europe. And in 1993 it is the *Año Santo* (Holy Year) in Spain, when Santiago de Compostela becomes an even more important place of Catholic pilgrimage than usual. These events have given lustre to Spain's new position at the centre of international culture, where it once gave a grand performance as the world's most powerful nation. They have also been the motor for massive changes

The grand approach to Palacio de Comunicaciones

affecting many aspects of Spanish life, and for an onward rush to the year 2000 which no other Western nation is experiencing. In the 1990s it is not military might which induces the world to remain attentive to Spanish affairs, but the attraction of its growing economic strength, its quiet diplomacy, and its vanguard position in humanity's intellectual and creative endeavours.

It is in Madrid, Spain's capital city, that the pulse of the New Spain is best felt, for Madrid is at the heart of Spain – geographically, politically and economically. A powerful king, Felipe II, put it there in the 16th century; and a 20th-century dictator, General Francisco

*Monument to
Columbus*

Franco, consolidated Madrid's centralist role
by basing his all-controlling bureaucracy here,
loading the city with head offices of banks and
other enterprises, and surrounding it with
industry. Since Spain's orderly progress to
democracy and political maturity, Madrid and
its province have become one of Spain's 17
Comunidades Autonomías (autonomous
regions), to which powers have been
devolved. Although cities like Barcelona,
Sevilla and Valencia have also blossomed
abundantly, as their political influence and
economies have grown, Madrid remains the
nation's pacesetter. And a fast pace it sets.
It was in Madrid that a cultural revival and
liberalised lifestyle known as *la Movida*
emerged from beneath the dampening blanket
of Francoism. The city's nomination as
European Cultural Capital for 1992 is an
impressive achievement: not only have there
been many infrastructural improvements, and
the opening of new venues and amenities;
there has also been a raising of cultural
awareness and access to culture. For its
visitors, too – rapidly gobbling culture vultures,
and those with serious interests and refined
tastes – Madrid offers a richly varied feast. The
Prado is among the world's foremost museums
of fine art; the Centro de Arte Reina Sofía is set
to be Europe's leading centre of contemporary
art; the performing arts have sparkling new or
renovated venues; and public and private
money supports an abundance of cultural
centres, where the plastic arts, music, drama
and education all flourish. In addition, a string
of festivals throughout the year celebrates
different forms of creative expression.
The city's many museums have collections that
enchant people of all ages and interests. Some
are housed in buildings as interesting as their
collections, and there are many other buildings
to appreciate which show a progression of
architectural styles, from medieval to modern.
Fascinating, too, is the distinctiveness of
Madrid's architecture, its urban arrangement
and atmosphere. Many delightful open spaces
offer escape from the noise of a city busily at
work, and there is a good choice of leisurely
diversions.

BACKGROUND

Orientation

There are three Madrids: the *Villa* (municipality), with an area of 234 square miles (606 sq km) and a population of 3.12 million, is Spain's capital city; the *Provincia* (province), covering 3,298 square miles (8,541 sq km), with close on 5 million people, is one of Spain's 50 provinces; and the *Comunidad*, which is the same as the province, forms one of Spain's 17 autonomous communities. Situated almost at the geographical centre of the country, on the *meseta*, a high central plain, Madrid is at the hub of Spain's communications network. The Sierra de Guadarrama mountains, which define the province in the northwest, provide climatic benefits as well as leisure amenities, which include resorts for wintersports. In the southwest are parts of the wooded Sierra de Somosierra and Gredos, to which *Madrileños* (Madriders) also escape on weekends and holidays. The Rio Tajo, the longest river in the Iberian peninsula, runs along the southern boundary of the province. Arable and stock farming takes place on the rolling plains covering most of the province.

Early Times

Around 180BC Celtiberian inhabitants of the area were subjugated by the Romans, who made their main settlement *Complutum* (Alcalá de Henares). This was inherited by the Visigoths when they assumed power in Spain during the 5th century. Combined Muslim forces (conveniently called Moors), invaded the peninsula in 711 and displaced the Visigoths. They were the first to consider the site of significance. Around 860 they built an *alcázar* (fort) above the Rio Manzanares where the Palacio Real now stands, which they named *Margerit*. Alfonso VI of Castile captured the Moorish settlement in 1083, and thereafter Christian orders were encouraged to establish communities there, fostering the growth of a *villa* (town). Moors came back to attack the settlement in 1109, and ever since then the area below the *alcázar* has been known as the Campo de Moro. Unlike the nearby cities of Avila, Segovia and Toledo,

BACKGROUND

Spanish rulers struggled against the Moors for centuries

Madrid does not have a legacy of notable medieval buildings – an indication of its low status during that period of history.

The subsequent story of Madrid is tied to that of Spain's rulers. Its rise to prominence began with *los Reyes Católicos* (the Catholic monarchs). In 1469 Aragón and Castile, the two Christian kingdoms of Spain, were united by marriage. Isabel (Isabella) I was crowned Queen of Castile in 1474, and Fernando (Ferdinand) II gained the throne of Aragón in 1479. They granted Madrid greater privileges, ordered the destruction of its medieval walls, and improved its urban arrangement. In the period of their joint rule (which lasted until Isabel's death in 1504), Granada, the last Moorish kingdom in the Peninsula, was captured; all Jews were expelled from Spain; and Colón (Columbus) reached the Americas. Fernando and Isabel also married their deranged daughter, Juana, to a son of the Habsburg Holy Roman Emperor, in a brilliant dynastic alliance.

The Habsburgs

Cardinal Cisneros, the favourite cleric of *los Reyes Católicos*, chose Madrid as his seat. When Fernando died in 1516, his teenage grandson, Carlos I, inherited the throne of a united Spain and its American colonies. Following the death of his paternal grandfather in 1519, Carlos gained the title Charles V, Holy Roman Emperor, and with it all the European territories of the Habsburgs (Germany, Austria, the Low Countries and parts of France). Some

communities, including Madrid, rose against
this 'foreign' ruler, but by 1521 Carlos had
subdued the revolt of the *comuneros*
(commoners) and instituted absolute rule. His
court was centred on Toledo, but during his
reign Madrid began to grow eastwards and
gained fine buildings, such as the Monasterio
de las Descalzas and the Casa de Cisneros.
Much of Spain's wealth from the Americas was
used in waging five wars against the French
and resisting the Protestant Reformation which
had started in Germany. In 1556, having given
the Austrian and German parts of the empire to
his brother, Carlos abdicated in favour of his
son, Felipe (Philip) II, and retired to a
monastery. Because of its central location,
abundance of water, equitable climate and
historic neutrality in disputes between the old
kingdoms of Christian Spain, Felipe
established Madrid as the nation's capital in
1561. From then onwards, Madrid's fortunes
entirely reflected those of Spain and its rulers,
inspiring a debate about the advantages and
disadvantages of being the capital which has
continued up to the present day. Soon the
spreading city was infamous as Europe's
dirtiest and most disease-ridden, and the
destruction of abundant forests near by, for fuel
and construction, began to produce adverse
effects on the local climate. Felipe's greatest
architectural bequest was the brooding mass
of El Escorial, Spain's biggest building, which
embodied his sombre personality. Felipe's
reign was marked by a campaign against the
Reformation in the Low Countries, the defeat of
the Turks at Lepanto (1571), the gaining of
Portugal (1581), and the failure of the Armada
against the English (1588). Before his death in
1598, he separated the Low Countries from
Spain by giving them to his daughter and her
Austrian husband.

During most of the reign of Felipe III
(1598–1621), the Duque de Lerma held
effective power. One of the duke's intrigues for
personal profit was to move the court to
Valladolid between 1601 and 1606; others
were to gain favour by creating more
aristocrats, and to please the Church by
founding more religious institutions. This gave

Felipe II, King of
Spain (1556–98)

BACKGROUND

Equestrian statue of Felipe IV

El Greco

Domenikos Theotokopulos was born in Crete in 1541, and before arriving in Spain in 1577 he worked in Italy under Titian and Tintoretto. He sought appointment as a court painter and obtained a commission in El Escorial. The king was not enthusiastic about his work and 'The Greek', settling in Toledo, made himself available for other commissions, mainly on religious themes. He repeated many of his subjects, and developed a unique style in which both his Italian training and Byzantine effects, such as the elongation of form and perspective, are strongly evident. His canvases of views and scenes are characterised by the use of vivid colours; often there are two compositions, such as an earthly scene below a heavenly vision, as in *El Entierro del Conde de Orgaz* (*The Burial of the Count of Orgaz*). Darker colours were used in portraits, usually showing subjects in reflective mood. There was no hint of his subsequent universal appreciation when El Greco died in 1614.

Madrid a boom in palaces and convents. While the national economy was foundering, the architect Juan Gómez de Mora (1585–1648) began to beautify the hastily built city with fine constructions, like the Plaza Mayor. Felipe IV (1621–65) was more attentive to national affairs, but relied on the Conde Duque de Olivares to direct them until 1643. Thereafter Felipe IV relied on the duke's nephew. Their schemes to regenerate the economy and make Spain an international power bore little fruit. Felipe's ordering of the huge Palacio del Buen Retiro, which was constructed in three years, drained his massive resources and symbolised the distance of the court from the nation. Most of the population, which had grown from 20,000 to 150,000 in a century, continued to live abject lives in the city's squalor.

Carlos II (1665–1700) was physically and mentally handicapped, and power was exercised by his mother, his half-brother and a council of nobles. During the reigns of the last three Habsburgs, Catalunya threatened secession, Portugal regained independence, Spain lost territories to the Dutch and French and some American colonies began to flex independent muscles. The century's political and economic malaise was countered by the creative vitality of a cultural golden age, *el Siglo de Oro*, to which artists like Velázquez and Murillo contributed.

Among the great writers of the period was Miguel de Cervantes Saavedra, born in Alcalá de Henares in 1547. He led an adventurous life, which included being wounded in the great naval battle of Lepanto (1571), followed by incarceration by Turks in Algiers for five years. He was also jailed for embezzlement at one point, when he was a tax collector. The first part of Saavedra's classic, *Don Quixote,* was published in 1605, the second in 1615. He died the following year, acclaimed for his work but still poor. Félix Lope de Vega (1562–1635) wrote some 1,500 works – *comedias* (a term which means both comedies and popular dramas), as well as religious dramas, short plays, ballads and sonnets – and was undoubtedly the world's most prolific dramatist. Madrid was also the home of two other great dramatists of the period: Tirso de Molina (1570–1648) who created Don Juan, and Pedro Calderón de la Barca (1600–1681), who portrayed Spain's declining power in a number of works.

The Bourbons

Before his death in 1700, childless Carlos II nominated Philipe, Duke of Anjou (a grandson of France's Louis XIV), as his successor. A rival claimant, Archduke Charles (who was heir to the Holy Roman Empire), had parts of Spain, like Catalunya, and most of Europe on his side. The War of the Spanish Succession ensued. It threw Europe into turmoil and ended in the Treaty of Utrecht of 1713, by which Philipe of Anjou became Felipe V, Spain's first Bourbon monarch. French styles and administrative methods became the order of the day in Spain, which remained embroiled in European conflicts for the rest of the 18th century. In and around Madrid the Bourbons indulged in a

BACKGROUND

Velázquez

Diego Velázquez was born in Sevilla in 1599
and at the age of 11 became a student of
Francisco Pachego, who was to become his
father-in-law. When he was 24 he moved to
Madrid and became court painter to Felipe IV,
a position he retained until his death in 1660.
Los Borrachos (The Drunkards) was the last
work painted in Velázquez's Sevilla style. From
1626 onwards his art showed a marked
transformation. This included a unique way of
dealing with aerial perspective, drawing the
viewer into the scene. This is superbly
exemplified in *Las Meninas*. The king,
members of the royal family, and courtiers,
among them dwarfs, were the main subjects of
Velázquez's paintings, along with mythological
and historical scenes. In them, naturalism
predominates and there is no strong
symbolism or propaganda.

Felipe IV on horseback, by Velázquez

passion for fine palaces. Felipe V ordered the
construction of the monumental Palacio Real
and the grand countryside retreat of La Granja.
A new architectural style, baroque, was given
lavish expression in public works by the
administrator and architect Pedro de Ribera
(1683–1742).

Fernando VI (1746–59) had a short,
unremarkable reign. That of his brother, Carlos
III (1759–88), was marked by the introduction
of a system of sewage and rubbish collection in
Madrid, which transformed the city into
Europe's cleanest capital. A programme of
urban improvement and embellishments also
took place, resulting in the construction of the
Plaza de la Cibeles. Able ministers such as
Aranda, Campomanes, Floridablanca and
Jovellanos, who are all commemorated today in
Madrid's public places, helped to give the
country a period of comparative prosperity.
There was violent resistance to some of the
decrees of the benign despot, Carlos III, who
favoured the neoclassical architect Juan de
Villanueva (1739–1811) with major
commissions. These included the Museo del
Prado.

Carlos IV (1788–1808) was well intentioned about reform and modernisation, but was less decisive than his predecessor had been. More so was his wife, Maria Luisa, and her favourite, the chief minister Manuel Godoy, who involved Spain in the affairs of revolutionary France. Napoleon's troops were allowed through Spain to attack Portugal, but mass protests caused the fall of Godoy and the abdication in March 1808 of Carlos in favour of his son, Fernando VII. The arrest of both the old and the new king of Spain by Napoleon caused another mass protest in Madrid on 2 May 1808. This was turned into a massacre on the orders of the French general, Murat. Pedro Velarde led the Spanish people in a spontaneous armed response, but French reprisals were severe. The *Dos de Mayo* (Second of May) is not forgotten in Madrid. Napoleon's brother was placed on the throne as José I, and the small town of Móstoles near Madrid was first to declare war on France. The Spanish War of Independence followed, supported by Britain. At Cádiz in 1812 the *Cortes* (Spanish parliament), adopted a liberal constitution, limiting the power of the king. By now Spain was rapidly losing most of its American colonies. On his return to resume the Bourbon throne in 1814, Fernando VII rejected the new constitution and all liberal aspirations, imposing general repression and strict censorship instead, and even reactivating the Inquisition. A revolt in 1820 enabled a liberal government to function until 1823, when Fernando was restored with French help. He resumed his autocratic rule until his death in 1833. Virtually the only good thing about him was that he founded the Prado Museum.

In 1833 Isabel II succeeded her father, Fernando VII. This was disputed by Don Carlos, her uncle, and led to the First and Second Carlist Wars (1833–5 and 1847–9). Spain then had a long period of political instability, with alternating liberal and conservative governments, appointed by *pronunciamientos* (uprisings) rather than elections. Isabel opted for exile in 1868. While the Third Carlist War (1872–6) was raging, Spain experimented briefly with its First

BACKGROUND

Goya

Francisco Goya was born in Aragón in 1746. He developed his artistic talents in Zaragoza and in Italy, and then in Madrid under Francisco Bayeu, his future brother-in-law. In 1755 Goya received an appointment at the Royal Tapestry Factory in Madrid, where he worked on many of his 'cartoons' as designs for tapestries. His reputation as a portrait painter gradually grew, and he began to work for leading families of Spain. In 1786 he was appointed court painter to Carlos III, a position he retained under Carlos IV and Fernando VII. His portrayals of the monarchs and their families are hardly flattering. A serious illness in 1792 with resultant deafness, and, perhaps, a difficult intimacy with the young Duchess of Alba, resulted in *los Caprichos*, a series of 80 satirical canvases completed in 1799. At this time Goya also completed *La Maja desnuda (The Naked Maja)* and *La Maja vestida (The Clothed Maja)*. The Duchess of Alba may have commissioned these works, but she was not the model for them, as has been widely believed. *El Dos de Mayo (The Second of May)* and *Los Fusilamientos en la Moncloa (The Executions of the Third of May)*, completed in 1814, dramatically record Madrid's uprising against the French in 1808, and a series of etchings, *Desastres de la Guerra* reflect on disasters of the subsequent war. In 1820 Goya began decorating his home with a series of saturnine murals, known as the *Pinturas Negras (Black Paintings)*. Goya rejected the absolutism and repression of Fernando VII and feared the Inquisition, which had declared *La Maja desnuda* obscene. In 1824 he took refuge in Bordeaux, where he died four years later. *La Lechera de Burdeos (The Milkmaid of Burdeos)* shows that he had lost none of his brilliance, even at the age of 81. Goya's remains were returned to Madrid in 1919 and interred in the church of San Antonio de la Florida, which he had decorated 121 years earlier with his inimitable frescoes. Goya was an exceptional chronicler of his time and the immense range of his work had an impact on both impressionists and expressionists.

Many works by Goya hang in the Prado

Republic. In 1875 the Bourbon line was restored, in the person of Alfonso XII, Isabel's son. Following his death in 1885, his posthumous son was proclaimed Alfonso XIII and Luisa Cristina, his wife, acted as regent until 1902. By 1898, after its war with the United States and Cuba, Spain had lost its colonial empire. General Primo de Rivera assumed dictatorial powers from 1923 to 1930, to which the king consented, but municipal elections in April 1931 gave supporters of a republic a big majority. Acceding to demands, Alfonso XIII abdicated. By December of that year, Alcalá Zamora had become president of Spain's Second Republic.

In Madrid the working class increasingly expressed itself through violent riots and industrial action, and adopted Marxist ideas. Spain's Socialist Workers' Party (the PSOE which governs today), was founded in an eating house near the Puerta del Sol at the end of the 1860s. Among café society there was much food for thought and intellectual discussion. The closing of religious houses, started by Fernando VII, had been virtually completed by 1836 under Mendizábal, a minister of state of Jewish origin, and the run-down palace and huge park of Buen Retiro had become public property. The Marqués de Salamanca, a property speculator who ended in ruin, laid out the extensive Salamanca district for the wealthy classes, which contrasted sharply with the poor areas of Chamberí, Inclusa, Universidad, Hospital and

Latina. In the last decades of the 19th century Ricardo Velázquez Bosco was the pre-eminent architect of the city, and the construction of Gran Via was a big project in the early 20th. Antonio Palacios, who was responsible for some buildings along the new broadway, had now become Madrid's leading architect.

Two novelists from other parts of Spain who spent their lives in Madrid provided vivid insights into the life of the times. Benito Pérez-Galdós (1843-1920) was Spain's greatest novelist since the *Siglo de Oro* (Golden Age) and his *Fortunata y Jacinta* is a vivid tapestry of characters. Another leading novelist at the turn of the century was the Basque, Pío Baroja (1872-1956), whose works show the life of Madrid's lower classes and reflect a national search for purpose and identity. Madrid was a creatively alive and stimulating place in the early decades of this century. At its university such diverse talents as Luis Buñuel (film-maker), Salvador Dalí (artist) and Federico García Lorca (poet) became close friends.

Civil War and Dictatorship

Widespread reforms, faction-fighting, incessant strikes and political chaos undermined the Second Republic. The imprisonment of José Antonio Primo de Rivera, son of the dictator and leader of the militant right-wing Falange organisation, coupled with the assasination of Calvo Sotelo, the monarchist leader, was the spark for an insurrection against the Popular Front government of Manuel Azaña on 17 July

Government forces taking prisoners during the Civil War

General Franco,
(1892–1975)

1936. It was started by General Francisco Franco in Morocco on that day. On 20 July a group of self-styled 'nationalists' who supported the rebellion were massacred at Madrid's Montaña military barracks, where the Templo de Debod now stands. By late October some 20,000 'nationalist' troops under Franco were on the outskirts of the city. Until 27 March 1939, *Madrileños* held out for the republic despite food shortages, bombardment, aerial bombing and the actions of murderous 'nationalists'. There were also disputes among the defending forces, which included volunteers from the International Brigade. Britain, France and the rest of the West did nothing to aid Spain's democratic government, whereas Hitler and Mussolini rehearsed for war by giving the rebels men and machines. After the Civil War, Franco (who assumed the title of Head of State in October 1936), dealt ruthlessly with republican prisoners. Many of them died building a hillside basilica which was to become Franco's mausoleum. From the Bourbon splendour of the Palacio de El Pardo, *el Generalísimo* ruled Spain and centralised political and economic power in Madrid. At the most beautiful building on the Puerta del Sol Franco's security police dealt with any opposition. Dull, pseudo-imperial architecture was a product of his stifling regime, but many *Madrileños* eager for privilege were won over by Franco's granting of favours to themselves or their city. New industries around Madrid attracted emigrants from poorer areas of Spain ,who greatly changed the city's demographic profile. In the 1960s Madrid's workers began tentative industrial action against the regime, and on Madrid's university campus students and riot police often battled. During this time an increasingly affluent middle class, millions of foreign tourists and international pressure began to have some effect in undermining the dictatorship, but Franco remained intransigent until his death on 20 November 1975.

Modern Bourbons and Democracy

Franco planned the restoration of the Spanish monarchy after his death. The dictator could not have guessed that King Juan Carlos I would nurture the nation to democracy through a new constitution, and that, with Queen Sofia, he would create a monarchy of almost universal popularity. Felipe, Príncipe de Asturias, born in 1966, is now heir to the throne; the Infantas Elena and Cristina are his sisters. Today the royal family lives in the modest Palacio de Zarzuela on the El Pardo estate, and the Palacio Real is only used on state occasions. The Palacio de Moncloa is the home and office of the *Presidente del Gobierno* (Prime Minister), and since 1982 it has been the domain of charismatic Felipe González, leader of the PSOE (Socialist Party). Spain's parliament, *las Cortes*, has two chambers: *el Congreso de los Diputados* (the Congress of Deputies) and *El Senado* (the Senate). Ministries are spread throughout the capital. Since the first elections for the *Comunidad Autónoma* (autonomous province) of Madrid in 1983, Joaquín Lequina, also of the PSOE, has been president of the regional government, and José María Alvarez del Manzano of the *Partido Popular* (Popular Party), Spain's main opposition group, became *alcalde* (mayor) of the city in 1991.

From the long night of dictatorship, Madrid awoke to the dawn of democracy and cast off the grey, wet blanket under which it had slumbered. *La Movida* was the name given to the city's explosive cultural and intellectual awakening, which made it a bright star attracting the best of Spain's talents. A galaxy of new venues, either for cultural appreciation or the sheer enjoyment of living, appeared. In the 1980s Madrid became, as it remains, one of the world's most animated and stimulating cities, appreciated by greatly increasing numbers of visitors. Madrid's modern architecture is only one expression of its regained confidence. ARCO, a huge contemporary art fair held each February, is another. The successful staging of the Middle East Peace Conference in Madrid in October 1991 also added to the city's prestige. As the capital of a country with rising cultural influence and international importance, Madrid enjoys a high profile today, and it has become one of the world's most expensive cities.

What to See

Madrid's principal sights are mostly concentrated within a few areas. You can get more from your time in Madrid, and avoid dashing around during sightseeing, by spending a little time planning your trip in advance. Experiencing Madrid does not only mean seeing as many of the sights listed in this section as possible; it also means enjoying different places to eat and drink, doing some shopping (window shopping, at least), experiencing the nightlife, or doing nothing more than spending time in a park and observing the locals. Later sections in this book will help you to gain experience of the city and its people.
Start by consulting the maps on pages 20–1, 22–3 and 36–7 of this book. Free ones are also available from tourist offices throughout the city, such as the *Plano Monumental* of Inprotur. More comprehensive *planos* (maps) with an A to Z *callejero* (street index) can be bought at kiosks and bookshops. The Puerta del Sol, the hub of public transport in the city, is the best point from which to get your bearings. West and southwest of Sol is the oldest part of the city – 'Asturias or Habsburg Madrid' – and such sights as the Palacio Real and Plaza Mayor. South and east of Sol, the enlivened *barrio* (district) of Cortés gives access to the Paseo del Prado, the grand boulevard of 'Bourbon Madrid'. Here the city's three great centres of art form a triangle, with the Parque del Retiro beyond. Continuing north from the Paseo del Prado, past the Plaza de la Cibeles and ending among the skyscrapers of 'Modern Madrid', is the long, wide north–south artery formed by the Paseo de la Recoletos and the Paseo de la Castellana, with the smart residential and shopping district of Salamanca to the east. North of Sol and beyond the broadway of Gran Vía, the *barrios* of Universidad and Justicia are a mix of notable buildings, student life, seediness, fashionable shopping and leisure. Gran Vía runs northwest to Plaza de España, beyond which are the shopping area of Argüelles and the delightful Parque de Oeste. West of here, across the canals of Rio

WHAT TO SEE

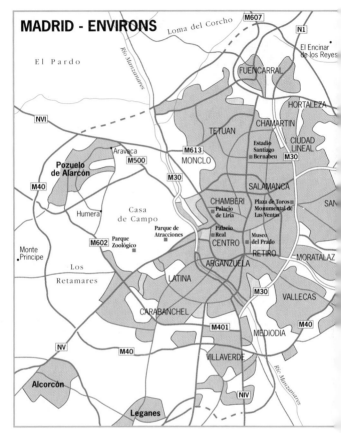

MADRID - ENVIRONS

Loma del Corcho

Río Manzanares

El Pardo

M607
N1
El Encinar
de los Reyes

FUENCARRAL

NVI

HORTALEZA

CHAMARTIN

Aravaca
Pozuelo
de Alarcón

TETUAN
M613
MONCLO
M500
M30

Estadio
Santiago
Bernabeu
CIUDAD
LINEAL
M30

SALAMANCA

M40

Humera

Casa
de Campo

CHAMBERI
Palacio
de Liria

Plaza de Toros
Monumental de
Las Ventas

SAN

Monte
Principe

Parque de
Atracciones

M602
Parque
Zoológico

Palacio
Real
CENTRO

Museo
del Prado
RETIRO

MORATALAZ

Los
Retamares

ARGANZUELA

LATINA

M30

VALLECAS

CARABANCHEL

M401
M40

NV
M40

MEDIODIA

VILLAVERDE

Río Manzanares

Alcorcón

NIV

Leganes

Manzanares, is the open
expanse of the Casa de
Campo.
Many of Madrid's sightseeing
highlights are in areas through
which the three **Walks in
Madrid** (pages 47–51), pass.
When planning your
sightseeing, read through the
Walks in Madrid section first,
and then refer back to
individual entries.
Many places of interest in

Madrid, and in the towns and
cities described in the
Excursions (pages 52–66) are
closed in the afternoon on
Sunday and public holidays,
and all day on Monday. An
important exception is the
Museo Nacional Centro de Arte
Reina Sofía which is open on
Monday but not Tuesday. As a
general guide, spend Sunday
in Madrid's markets and open
spaces, and on Monday go

Personal Safety

As in any big city, take this subject seriously. The simplest rule is not to dress and behave like a tourist: like wearing blatantly foreign clothes, bedecking yourself with cameras, flapping maps around and arguing loudly with a companion about what to do next. Instead, carry a copy of a local daily paper, such as *El Pais,* with you and keep your guidebook and map hidden. (See also Crime in the **Directory**.) A special hazard for Madrid's visitors is the wide avenues with many lanes of traffic, as well as the alarming habits of some drivers. They have an obvious dislike of traffic lights, either because of macho defiance, or from utter frustration with the city's traffic congestion, and whenever an opportunity arises they emulate Spain's rally star, Carlos Sainz. At pedestrian crossings, stand back from the kerb. Cross on the green light *only* after you have checked that oncoming traffic in all lanes has stopped.

shopping.

Madrid is a very dynamic city with constantly changing things to see and do. Its celebration as European Cultural Capital in 1992 included the announcement, in May, of the move of Picasso's *Guernica* to the Museo Nacional Centro de Arte Reina Sofia, and the opening in October of the Thyssen Collection in the Palacio de Villahermosa. Some projects, however, have been seriously delayed; others are planned but may not come to fruition. It is essential to refer to local media listings for current information, and to make enquiries at one of the tourist offices (see **Directory**). Although the permanent collections of some museums may not appeal to you, you might find temporary showings at the time of your visit that do.

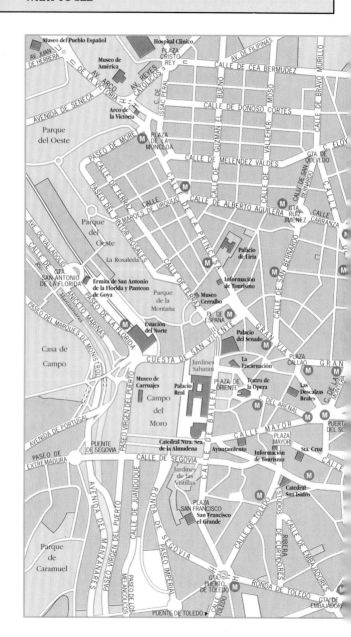

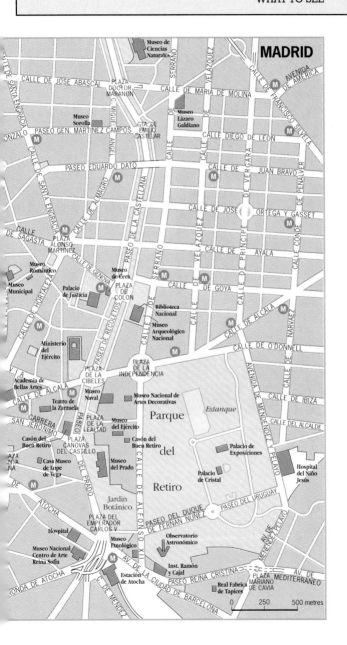

Cervantes Monument

WHAT TO SEE

◆
CAMPO DE LAS NACIONES
off N II, Carretera Barcelona
In the northeast of the city, this large-scale development project, partly opened in 1992, is going to become a new focus of interest. Extensive, ultra-modern installations will cater for the city's continuous programme of trade and other fairs for professionals and the public. Madrid has gained a new venue for concerts and other spectaculars here in the 25,000-seat **Auditorio del Parque de las Hinojosa**. The **Jardín de las Tres Culturas** was designed by the Argentinian landscape artist Myriam Silber Brodsky to commemorate Christian, Jewish and Muslim cultures, suggesting Paradise and possible unity. A large sculpture, *El Arbol de la Vida* (The Tree of Life) is the park's centrepiece.

◆◆◆
CASA DE AMERICA
Plaza de la Cibeles
The public authorities have invested 6,000 million pesetas in the acquisition and restoration of the **Palacio de Linares**, now to be found in the Casa de America building. The *palacio* was built in 1875 to designs by the Frenchman Ombreton. Although considered one of the city's grandest palaces, it fell into disrepair, and its restoration by architect Carlos Puente and restorer María Alvarez Garcillán

Among the many venues for interesting events or showings, it is usually worthwhile to see what is on at: **Círculo de Bellas Artes**, Alcalá 42; **Fundación Caja de Pensiones**, Serrano 60; **Fundación Juan March**, Castelló 77; **Fundación Mapfre Vida**, Avenida del General Perón 40; and **Sala de Exposiciones de la Consejería de Cultura de la Comunidad de Madrid**, Plaza de España 8.

is considered one of the most important ever undertaken in Spain. The palace shows an eclectic mix of late-19th-century tastes – from Chinese to Pompeiian, Byzantine and Spanish Renaissance. Its part-opening in late July 1992 coincided with the meeting in Madrid of the *II Cumbre Iberoamericana* (11th Latin-American Summit). The Casa de América is to be a cultural, diplomatic and institutional centre for relations between Spain and Latin America. Also installed is the **Museo de América**, with a wide-ranging collection covering pre-conquest times and the period of the conquest, as well as scientific expeditions of the 18th and 19th centuries.
Open: Check locally.
Metro: Banco.

◆◆
CASA DE CAMPO
On the western outskirts of the city, across the Rio Manzanares, is one of Europe's largest urban parks with an area of 4,317 acres (1,747 hectares). Felipe II first acquired wooded land here for use as a royal hunting reserve, and successive monarchs added to its size. Isabel II and the regent María Cristina improved the forestation, and it ceased to be a place for privileged hunters. In 1931 it was ceded to the *Ayuntamiento* (municipality) and it became a recreation area for *Madrileños*. Now, on Sundays and holidays in warm weather, some half a million people come here, some in the 50,000 cars which pack the park. Many use

the *teleférico* (cable car) and enjoy a grand panorama of the city and surroundings. It is a pleasant area in which to walk, have a picnic or patronise installations, which include Madrid's Zoo, a pleasure lake, an amusement park, bars and restaurants.
Metro: Lago, Batán.

◆◆
CENTRO CULTURAL DE CONDE DUQUE
Conde Duque
One of Madrid's recently acquired cultural venues is housed in a part of the imposingly austere *cuartel* (barracks) of Felipe V's bodyguard, which was completed in 1753 following plans of Pedro de Ribera. It is worth visiting just to see the successful renovation of what was a decaying building, and it is always worth checking what exhibitions or live shows are on.
Metro: Ventura Rodríguez, Plaza de España.

◆◆
CENTRO CULTURAL DE LA VILLA
Plaza de Colón
Below a neo-Gothic column and statue of Cristóbal Colón (Christopher Columbus) raised in 1885, this subterranean cultural venue sponsored by the *Ayuntamiento* (Council of Madrid) has been an important scene in the capital's cultural reawakening since it opened in 1977. Visitors should find out what is being presented here during their time in the city. Also on the *plaza* are the Jardines del Descubrimiento.
Metro: Colón.

WHAT TO SEE

♦♦♦
ERMITA DE SAN ANTONIO DE LA FLORIDA Y PANTEON DE GOYA

Glorieta de San Antonio de Florida

The building of the church by Italian architect Francisco Fontana started in 1792, and in 1798 the Court Painter, Francisco de Goya, completed its exceptional series of secular frescoes, which gave both the church and Goya great fame.

Goya gave vent to his cynical attitude towards the Church by including ladies of ill repute among the figures of angels and people at court in the frescoes adorning the cupola. San Antonio is portrayed raising a murdered man from the dead, so that he can name his murderer and save an innocent who stands accused of the crime.

The building, situated on the banks of the Manzanares, was declared a national monument in 1905 and in 1919 Goya's remains were interred here. In 1928 the church opened as a museum after restoration by the *Sociedad de Amigos de las Bellas Artes* (Society of Fine Art Lovers) and the building of a replica parish church. The room with Goya's drawings, engravings and some personal objects was installed in 1977, making this even more an essential place for admirers of the artist to visit.

Open: Tuesday to Friday 10.00–15.00 and 16.00–20.00hrs; Saturday and Sunday 10.00–14.00hrs.
Metro: Plaza de España.

♦♦♦
MONASTERIO DE LAS ✓ DESCALZAS REALES

Plaza de las Descalzas 3

Doña Juana, a sister of Felipe II, had a palace converted into a religious house for women of the court who took up residence in 1559. Claudio Coello was principally responsible for the rich adornment of the walls and ceilings, most notable in the **Salón de los Reyes** and **Sala de Tapices**. As a monastery it was richly endowed with paintings by Rubens, Murillo, Zurbarán and others, as well as many sculptures, among which works by Pedro de Mena are prominent. In the **Relicario** room is a wealth of gold and silverwork, jewellery, relics and liturgical pieces. Since 1960 the public has been allowed to see some of the rooms and their collections on conducted visits.

Open: Tuesday to Saturday 10.30–12.30 and 16.00–17.30hrs; Sunday 11.00–13.30hrs.
Metro: Sol, Opera, Callao.

♦♦♦
MONASTERIO DE LA ✓ ENCARNACION

Plaza de la Encarnación

Building began in 1616 under the auspices of Felipe III, as a gesture to his wife Margarita. Felipe IV continued with its endowment. An underground passage linked it with the royal palace so that nuns and ladies of royal blood could avoid being seen in public. Juan Gómez de

Mora is credited as the principal architect; Ventura Rodríguez directed the rebuilding of the church in the 18th century, and it is richly decorated with works of artists and craftsmen of that time. Rooms of the convent have a collection of fine works by lesser-known artists and sculptors. In an elaborately adorned chapel, the **Relicario** displays a wealth of religious art and craftsmanship as well as a crystal of the blood of San Pantaleón, which turns to liquid on 26 July.
Open: 10.00–13.00 and 16.00–17.30hrs; mornings only on Monday, Friday and Sunday. *Metro*: Opera.

◆◆◆
MUSEO DE LA ACADEMIA DE BELLAS ARTES DE SAN FERNANDO
Alcalá 13
Art lovers should not miss this rewarding museum, which tends to be overshadowed by the glamour and events of those within the 'art triangle'. Some of the finest works of the Real Academia de Bellas Artes,

Monasterio de las Descalzas: the façade

WHAT TO SEE

Inside the Museo de Bellas Artes

founded in 1752, were transferred to the Prado in 1902. Recent modernisation has greatly improved the display of the remaining collection, which after that of the Prado contains some of the best examples of Spanish art from the 16th and 19th centuries, including works by the 'greats' – El Greco, Velázquez and Goya. Foreign masters are represented with works by Rubens and Van Dyck, among others. The **Calcografía Nacional** displays printing plates and engravings of the 18th-20th centuries, and sells prints. The original building, completed in 1710, was planned by Churriguera; Juan de Villanueva made later alterations,
Open: Tuesday to Saturday 09.00–19.00hrs; Sunday and Monday 09.00–14.00hrs.
Metro: Sevilla, Sol.

♦♦♦
MUSEO ARQUEOLOGICO ✓ Y BIBLIOTECA NACIONAL

Serrano 13
For some people the museum is easily rated on a par with the Prado as the prime place in Madrid at which to spend time, but its visitor count is considerably lower. Isabel II founded the National Archaeological Museum in 1867, and it was installed here in 1895. Thirty years earlier Francisco Jareño had planned the large quadrilateral building with two principal façades: on Calle Serrano and on Paseo de Recoletos. Because of the elevation of its central portico, the latter front is more impressive. The building includes the **Biblioteca Nacional** (National Library), and it is worth checking what there is to see in its newly renovated exhibition areas. The archaeological museum's main collection is immensely varied and rich. It presents a fascinating display of the evolution of creativity and artistic endeavour in the Iberian peninsula, and in other Mediterranean areas, from prehistory to this century. Descriptions of the exhibits are given only in Castilian, however, so visitors are advised to buy a current edition of the catalogue which is available in other languages. At the main entrance is an underground replica of the lifelike ochre paintings, dating from around 12,000BC, of the *Cuevas de Altamira* (Caves of Altamira) in Cantabria. Briefly,

the museum's collection includes a broad range of pieces from the Paleolithic, Bronze and Iron Ages; from the cultures of the Iberian and Etruscan peoples of Spain and Italy; and from widely spread Phoenician, Greek and Carthaginian (Punic) communities. The Roman section has sculptures, mosaics and other ceramics, as well as architectural remains. The Visigoth occupation of the peninsula is represented by the best collection of their art anywhere. It includes the golden *Tesoro de Guarrazar* (Treasure of Guarrazar), including six crowns and several crosses. Muslim art and architecture are broadly covered, and exhibits include instruments and works in bronze, showing delicate craftsmanship. Christian Spain's Romanesque, Gothic, Renaissance and baroque periods are also well represented. A numismatic collection covers the centuries, but greatest reverence is probably paid to the museum's three fine *Damas* (Ladies), splendid Iberian sculptures of women named after the places where they were found: Elche, Baza and Cerro de los Santos. *Open:* Tuesday to Sunday 09.15–13.45hrs.
Metro: Serrano, Colón.

◆
MUSEO CERRALBO
Ventura Rodríguez 17
The private collection of the 17th Marqués de Cerralbo, who died in 1922, is displayed in his small palace dating from

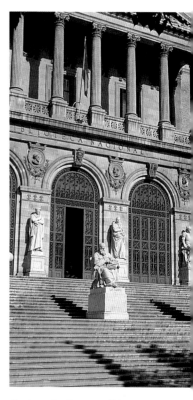

The imposing frontage of Museo Arqueologico and Biblioteca Nacional

1884. It includes paintings, sculptures, tapestries, armour, glassware and furniture. Among paintings are works by El Greco, Zurbarán, Tintoretto and Ribera, and there are sketches and designs by Goya and Mengs among others.
Open: Tuesday to Sunday 10.00–15.00hrs; closed in August.
Metro: Plaza de España, Ventura Rodríguez.

WHAT TO SEE

♦♦♦
MUSEO LAZARO GALDIANO ✓

Serrano 122
José Lázaro Galdiano (1862–1947) was a writer and publisher of some influence in Spanish cultural life. He was also a magpie collector of wide interests and great discrimination, who bequeathed his enchanting small palace, set in a pleasant garden, with all it held, to the state. In 1951 it opened as a museum. Visitors to Madrid should try not to miss it. It is advisable to buy a guide to appreciate the collection; the museum also publishes *Goya*, the respected art review magazine. Almost all the great Spanish masters are represented by paintings: Berruguette, Claudio Coello, Goya, El Greco, Murillo, Ribera, Velázquez and Zurbarán. A strong selection of English painters includes Constable, Gainsborough, Reynolds and Turner. There is an *Ecce Homo* of Bosch, and a work attributed to Leonardo da Vinci, *La Cabeza del Salvador* (*The Head of the Saviour*). More varied paintings of earlier and later dates, bronzes and other sculptures (including a terracotta bust of Christ by Verrocchio), furniture and many decorative pieces feature among the larger items. Among the smaller ones are ivories, enamelwork, ceramics, glassware, fans, jewellery, clocks, clothing and all sorts of miniatures. It is difficult to imagine the time spent by Don José in achieving his eclectic assembly; but it is easy, delightful and very educational to see it.
Open: Tuesday to Sunday 10.00–14.00hrs; closed in August. *Metro*: Rubén Darío, Núñez de Balboa.

♦
MUSEO MUNICIPAL
Fuencarral 78
In 1726 Pedro de Ribera completed the **Hospice de San Fernando** in a pure expression of Madrid's baroque style. The elaborate portal with the statue of San Fernando is the work of sculptor Juan Ron. The museum's exhibits – maps and models – show the city's growth.
Open: Check locally; the new Museo de la Ciudad is being installed near the Auditorio Nacional on Calle Príncipe de Vergara. *Metro*: Tribunal.

♦
MUSEO NACIONAL DE ARTES DECORATIVAS
Montalbán 12
Surprisingly, in Spain's National Museum of Decorative Arts there is a worthy collection of art from the Far East. More to be expected is the museum's good selection of ceramics from different parts of Spain, and its collection of glass dating from Phoenician times to today. There are also varied exhibits of furniture, wood sculpture and religious art. The museum was created in 1912 and is housed in a 19th-century palace.
Open: Tuesday to Friday 09.30–14.30hrs; Saturday and Sunday 10.00–14.00hrs.
Metro: Retiro, Banco.

◆◆◆
MUSEO NACIONAL ✓ CENTRO DE ARTE REINA SOFIA

Santa Isabel 52
It has not been an easy task to convert a huge 18th-century public hospital into one of Europe's most vibrant centres for recent and contemporary creativity; a rival to New York's MOMA. Controversy has attended every step on the difficult road since the opening of the renovated building as a centre for the arts in November 1990. Early in the next year it had a new director, María Corral, who called her job creating a museum 'a great adventure, in which the whole of Spanish society should be involved'. Although she also said that 'museums are not made overnight', there was a long delay in announcing the contents of the museum's permanent collection; this was not confirmed until mid–1992. In May, the Reina Sofía's future as a crowd-puller was assured with the announcement that it was to receive Picasso's *Guernica* from the Prado. Guernica is a Basque town, which was strafed and bombed for Franco by Hitler's airforce during the Spanish Civil War. Picasso's huge canvas, which is both a memorial and a political statement, with powerful images in muted tones, was made for the pavilion of Spain's Republican Government at the Paris World Fair of 1937. In 1981, the centenary of Picasso's birth, the painting was brought to Spain from New York's MOMA. The artist's many preliminary drawings can also be seen.

Some 3,000 paintings, sculptures and drawings were acquired from the old **Museum of Contemporary Art**, of which only around 200 are shown at a time. They form the bedrock of the permanent collection, which is based on Spanish art and its international context, from the vanguard work of Picasso, Dalí, Gris and Miró to that of the 1980s, including artists like Tápies, Saura and López. There is emphasis on works of recent years, when Spain once again become integrated into the

Photography on display at Museo Reina Sofía

WHAT TO SEE

wider art world.
Much of the Reina Sofía's 135,000
square feet (12,555sq m) of
exhibition space, some 40 per
cent of the building, is allocated
to temporary showings
covering the plastic arts.
Adding to the interest are
music, theatre, readings,
lectures, courses and other
events. A cafeteria, terraces
and a good shop complement
the offer.
Francisco Sabatini designed
the building, formerly the
Hospital de San Carlos, in 1776.
He could not have imagined
today's perspex-enclosed lifts
on the outside of the building.
Open: Wednesday to Monday
10.00–21.00hrs; Sunday
10.00–14.30hrs. *Metro*: Atocha.

◆

MUSEO NACIONAL DE
CIENCAS NATURALES
Paseo de la Castellana 80
There are well arranged,
interesting displays covering
palaeoanthropology, zoology,
entomology, geology and
mineralogy. Favourites are the
models of huge animals and the
world's best-known diamonds.
Open: Tuesday to Saturday
09.00–14.00 and 15.00–18.00hrs.
Metro: Buevos Ministerios.

◆

MUSEO NACIONAL DE
ETNOLOGIA
Alfonso XII 68
The building and core of the
collection date from 1875 and
there is a fascinating mixed
to be seen from around the
world.
Open: Tuesday to Sunday
10.00–18.00hrs; Sunday
10.00–14.00hrs. *Metro:* Atocha.

◆◆◆
MUSEO NACIONAL
DEL PRADO

Paseo del Prado
Carlos III's commission in 1785
for a natural history museum,
library and academy gave Juan
de Villanueva the opportunity
to design what is the finest
neoclassical building in Spain.
At his wife's suggestion
Fernando VII ordered the
assembly here, in 1819, of the
vast royal art collection which
Carlos V had begun. The
dissolution of many religious
institutions in the 19th century
added many more works of
great merit to it. The collection
was also enriched by valuable
bequests and purchases over
the years. Today the Prado
ranks among the world's
richest art galleries, and it is the
most-visited museum in Spain,
attracting 1.5 million people in
1991. Only about half of its
6,000 paintings is on exhibition
at any time. In recent years
extensive modifications have
improved the main building as
a museum of art. Use has also
been made of the **Casón del
Buen Retiro** and of the **Palacio
de Villanueva** (now the **Museo
Thyssen-Bornemisza**).
Announcements in the summer
of 1992 promised significant
enhancements of the Prado's
amenities and its ability to show
more of its collection: the
Casón del Buen Retiro will be
remodelled, and may house a
monographic Goya museum;
what was formerly the
Ministerio de Agricultura will
become an annexe of the
Prado; and the fine building in

Museo del Prado

which the **Museo de Ejército** has been housed also features in the Ministry of Culture's plans for use by the Prado. The Prado will also have the use of the **Palacio de Velázquez** in the Parque del Retiro.
Visitors should check the situation regarding layout on arrival. A quick visit to the museum will indicate its size and scope; but it is advisable to make a number of visits, concentrating on specific areas of interest, to avoid over-saturation. It is also well worthwhile buying an up-to-date guide to the museum.
The Prado's greatest strength lies in its assembly of works from Spain's Golden Age – El Greco, Valdés Leal, Alonso Cano, Murillo, Zurbarán, Ribera, Ribalta and Velázquez among them – and in having the most representative collection of Goya's works.
Among earlier works of

Spanish art are Romanesque murals, plus works by Pedro Berruguette, Luis de Morales and Sánchez Coello. There is also a collection of 19th-century Spanish art, covering portraiture, the followers of the Romantic School, landscapes, impressionists (like Sorolla and Fortuny) and Catalan modernists (Casas and Rusinyol).
Spain's earlier kings were great admirers of Italian painters, and among the many Italian works are paintings by Raphael, Fra Angélico, Botticelli and Mantegna, as well as those of the Venetian School (Titian, Tintoretto and Tiépolo).
Flanders once belonged to Spain and among the Flemish masters are Bosch, Rubens and Van Dyck. There are also works of great Dutch, English, French and German painters,

WHAT TO SEE

including Rembrandt,
Gainsborough, Poussin and
Mengs. An important collection
of classical sculpture mainly
originates from collections
gathered by Queen Christina of
Sweden in the 17th century,
and by José Azara, Spain's
ambassador in Rome, during
the late-18th century.
There is a pleasant cafeteria
and a well-stocked shop.
Open: Tuesday to Saturday
09.00–19.00hrs; Sunday
09.00–14.00hrs.
Metro: Banco, Atocha.

MUSEO NAVAL
Paseo del Prado 5
It displays models, maps,
paintings, papers and
publications relating to naval
matters generally, and to
Spain's navy directly. Juan de
Cosa's world map of 1500 was
the first to show the American
continent.
Open: Tuesday to Sunday
10.30–13.30hrs.
Metro: Banco.

◆◆
MUSEO DEL PUEBLO
ESPAÑOL
Avenida Juan de Herrera 12
After the remodelling has taken
place of what was formerly the
home of the Museum of
Contemporary Art, the
Museum of the Spanish People
will show a comprehensive
collection of clothing, furniture,
ceramics, textiles, musical
instruments and other items
reflecting the country's wide-
ranging popular arts and
regional diversity.
Open: Check locally.
Metro: Moncloa.

MUSEO ROMANTICO
San Mateo 13
An elegant mansion houses an
evocative collection of the
Romantic period established by
the Marqués de la Vega-Inclan.
Open: Tuesday to Sunday
10.00–15.00hrs; closed in
August. *Metro:* Tribunal.

◆◆
MUSEO SOROLLA
*Paseo General Martínez
Campos 37*
The Valencian painter of
impressionist tendency,
Joaquín Sorolla (1863–1923),
had this house built in 1910.
Few changes were made for its
conversion into a charming
museum, which today gives an
intimate insight into the lifestyle
of the artist and his family, and
into the development of his art.
Open: Tuesday to Sunday
10.00–14.00hrs; closed in
August.
Metro: Rubén Darío, Iglesia.

◆◆◆
MUSEO THYSSEN-BORNEMISZA ✓

Paseo del Prado 8
When Baron Heinrich Thyssen declared that he wanted to move his art collection from Switzerland to a new home, many countries were very eager to have what is widely considered as the second most important private collection in the world after that of Queen Elizabeth II. Spain had an advantage in that the Baroness Thyssen (Carmen Cervera) is Spanish, and was keen to have the collection moved to Madrid. Spain also made a generous financial offer of 9,000 million pesetas to the Fundación Thyssen-Bornemisza to receive the collection for 9½ years. Some 4,000 million pesetas, double the 1988 estimates, have been spent in turning the neoclassical **Palacio de**

Villahermosa, one of the city's best-looking buildings, into a modern museum. It follows the designs of architect Rafael Moneo and the tastes of the Baroness. Around 65,000 square feet (6,045sq m), about one third of the building, is given to exhibition space for the permanent collection and changing showings. In October 1992 the museum opened with the latest technology and security; 51 rooms have pale terracotta walls and marble floors, and the aim has been to make them welcoming and permit an untiring progress through them all. There are some 800 works on view in the collection. Broadly, the division is as follows: lower floor – vanguard artists of the 20th century, with some works of the 1980s; first floor – Dutch paintings of the 17th century and English and American works from the 19th; and second floor – masters up to the 18th century, as well as various sculptures, ceramics, jewellery and ivories. Among the big names are Cranach, Holbein, Raphael, Rubens, Hals, Renoir, Degas, Monet, Van Gogh, Cézanne, Picasso, Gris, Leger, Mondrian, Miró and Hopper. With the third point in its glorious 'art triangle' now completed, Madrid is a cultural capital of universal stature and appeal.
Open: check locally.
Metro: Banco.

Flamenco dancing is one of Spain's oldest and most popular art forms

CENTRAL MADRID

Parque del Oeste
Templo de Debod
Jardines Ferraz
Parque da la Montaña
Estación del Norte
Campo del Moro

Palacio de Liria
Centro Cultural de Conde Duque
Iglesia de Montserrat
Santos Justo y Pastor
Información de Turismo
Museo Cerralbo
San Marcos
PLAZA DE ESPAÑA
S.Placido
S Martín
Palacio del Senado
PLAZA MARINA ESPAÑOLA
PLAZA SANTO DOMINGO
JACOME TREZO
PLAZA CALLAO
Jardines Sabatini
La Encarnación
Jardines Cabo Noval
PLAZA CARMEN
Palacio Real o de Oriente
PLAZA DE ORIENTE
Teatro de la Opera (Teatro Real)
PLAZA ISABEL II
Las Descalzas Reales
PLAZA DE LA ARMERIA
Santiago
PUERTA DEL SOL
Policia
Catedral Nuestra Señora de la Almudena
PLAZA SANTIAGO
San Nicolas
Torre de los Lujanes
PLAZA C MORENAS
MAYOR
Casa de Cisneros
PLAZA DE LA VILLA
Mercado de San Miguel
PLAZA MAYOR
Iglesia de San Miguel
Información de Turismo
Sta Cruz
PL. JACINTO BENAVENTE
Jardines de las Vistillas
PL GABRIEL MIRO
Plazuela del Cordón
San Pedro
PL SEGOVIA NUEVA
CONCEPCION JERONIMA
San Andrés y Capilla del Obispo
PL. HUMILLADERO
Catedral San Isidro
PL TIRSO DE MOLINA
PLAZA SAN FRANCISCO
San Francisco el Grande
Mercado de la Cebada
San Cayetano
GTA PUERTA DE TOLEDO

0   200 metres

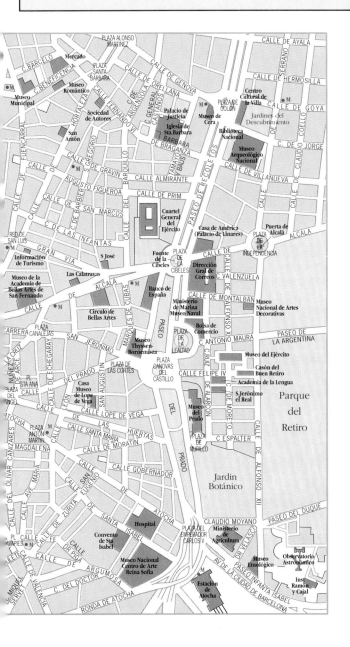

WHAT TO SEE

◆
PALACIO DE LIRIA
Princesa 20
Ventura Rodríguez completed this fine palace in the 1770s and it is now the home in Madrid of the Alba family. Badly damaged during the Civil War, it was rebuilt in the 1950s. The rich private collection, including works by El Greco, Velázquez, Titian and Rubens, may be seen on Saturday mornings by appointment (tel: 247 5302).
Metro: Plaza de España.

Corinthian columns and a balustrade adorn Palacio Real

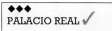

◆◆◆
PALACIO REAL ✓

Bailén
Around 1465 a royal palace had been built on the site of the earlier Arab *alcázar*. Accustomed to greater splendour, the Bourbon Felipe V ordered the building, in 1737, of the Palacio de Oriente there, to plans of Juan Bautista Sachetti. Francisco Sabatini and Ventura Rodríguez also worked on the project, which was completed in 1764 for Carlos III. Giaquinto, Mengs, Tiépolo, González, Velázquez and Francisco Bayeu were principal contributors to the elaborate

decoration. Outside, the lower stonework is of granite from the Sierra de Guadarrama, while the upper stories are of white Colmenar stone. Because of the sloping ground, the most impressive aspects are from the north (Jardines de Sabatini) and west (Campo de Moro). Wings of some 460 feet (140m) surround a central square; on the south side two lateral wings flank the **Plaza de Armas**, where visitors enter. Conducted tours are made through rooms where all the sumptuousness of an extravagant royalty's principal palace, accentuated by Bourbon tastes, is to be

experienced, together with a rich and varied collection of the finest art, tapestry, furniture, porcelain, glass, clocks, etcetera. The **Biblioteca Real** has some 300,000 volumes and 4,000 manuscripts; the **Armeria Real** is loaded with the shining armour and lethal arms of kings and nobles. All in all it is a mind-boggling and neck-straining experience, but well worth the endurance.
Open: 09.30–12.00 and 16.00–17.15hrs; Sunday and holidays 09.30–13.30hrs; closed during official functions.
Metro: Opera.

◆◆
PARDO, EL
off N VI, on Carretera El Pardo (see map on pages 20 and 21)
On the northwest outskirts of the city, this high area was once a large royal estate covered with forests of holm oaks and other trees. It is still pleasantly wooded in parts, and a visit gives some respite from the city's bustle and noise. Within the area is the **Palacio de Zarzuela**, the fairly modest home of Spain's royal family. The first Palacio de El Pardo was built in the 15th century as a summer palace, but there has been much rebuilding and remodelling, following fires and changing tastes. What now stands reflects the desires of Fernando VI, Carlos III and Carlos IV, and is principally the work of Francisco Sabatini.
Following the Civil War, Franco made this palace his residence, and today it is a guest house for state visitors.
In 1784 **La Casita del Príncipe**

A tranquil scene in Parque del Retiro

was designed by Juan de Villanueva as a recreation lodge for the crown prince, later Carlos IV. It was richly decorated and, after falling into disrepair, was faithfully restored in the 1950s. *Open*: Monday to Saturday 10.00–13.00 and 15.30–18.00hrs; Sunday 10.00–13.00hrs; closed afternoons (La Casita), and when state guests are in residence (Palacio). *Bus*: *83* from Paseo de Moret/Calle Princesa.

◆◆◆
PARQUE DEL RETIRO
Alcalá, Alfonso XII, Avenida Menéndez Pelayo

Madrid is well endowed with green spaces and since it was opened to the public in the last century this has been the *Madrileños'*, favourite place in which to parade and indulge in people-watching. It has different aspects in its various parts. Central features are the *estanque* (lake), on which people play in boats, and the huge monument to Alfonso XII, inaugurated in 1922. Not to be missed for their architecture, or

for any exhibitions they may be hosting, are the **Palacios de Cristal y Velázquez**. Ricardo Velázquez Bosco was the architect of both buildings. The former, built in 1886 and intended as a greenhouse, is an outstanding example of refined iron architecture; the latter, dating from 1883, incorporates walls of two-coloured brick with ironwork. The glazed tiles in both buildings are by the painter Daniel Zuloaga. (See also the section on **Children**.)
Metro: Retiro, Banco.

◆
PARROQUIA DE SAN ANDRES Y CAPILLA DE SAN ISIDRO
Puerta de Moros
Two notable architectural examples are found in this parish church dating from the late-16th century: the **Capilla del Obispo** is Madrid's only remaining Gothic structure, while the **Capilla de San Isidro** is a baroque addition from the mid-17th century, for which stones from Madrid's medieval walls were used.
Metro: La Latina.

◆◆◆
PASEOS DEL PRADO, DE RECOLETOS, DE LA CASTELLANA
Visitors to Madrid are unlikely to miss these wide boulevards which, from Glorieta de Emperador Carlos V in the south, to Plaza de Castilla in the north, make up the city's main north–south artery. In the warm season they are enlivened by some 40 *terrazas* (terraces). Most are pleasantly tree-shaded and the most elegant is

the **Paseo del Prado**, between the Glorieta and Plaza de la Cibeles. Besides the great museums, fine hotels and other notable buildings (see **Walk 3**), the Paseo del Prado is graced by two fountains planned by Ventura Rodríguez: **Fuente de Apolo** and **Fuente de Neptuno**. Modern buildings mix with private palaces converted to other uses along the Paseo de Recoletos, and lower parts of Paseo de la Castellana. Near Plaza de Colón, where two tall modern towers rise, Recoletos is dominated by the imposing front of the **Biblioteca Nacional**. Where Calle Eduardo crosses Castellana, the **Museo de Escultura al Aire Libre** displays modern works in stone, concrete and metals, including pieces by Miró and Chillida. Beyond **Nuevos Ministerios,** a block of government buildings designed before the Civil War and completed in the 1950s, Castellana cuts through Modern Madrid. The **Banco de Bilbao** (number 79–81), was designed by Sáenz de Oiza and is generally considered the city's most outstanding example of contemporary architecture. **Torre Picasso** in Plaza de Picasso is Madrid's tallest building, and was designed by the Japanese architect Yamasaki.

◆◆◆
PLAZA DE LA CIBELES
The statue of the frigid goddess Cibeles on a chariot drawn by lions was designed by Ventura Rodríguez to be part of the

WHAT TO SEE

embellishment of the Paseo del Prado in the 1780s. It was moved to its location at the centre of this busy traffic circle in 1895, and has become one of the symbols of the city. Paseos del Prado and Recoletos link here with Calle Alcalá. The white confection of the **Palacio de Comunicaciones**, completed in 1917, was a work of Palacios and Otamendi. Begun in 1891, the **Banco de España** shows an eclectic style, including some Renaissance ideas and a roof of French influence. The **Cuartel General del Ejército** (army headquarters) occupies the Palacio de Buenavista, built in the late-18th century. Across the Paseo de Recoletos is the splendidly reformed **Palacio de Linares** (see **Casa de América**).
Metro: Banco.

♦♦
PLAZA DE ESPAÑA
Entered by Gran Vía and Calle Princesa on the northeast, and bordered by Calle Bailén on the west, this is a large open space of concrete and gardens, at whose centre the bronze figures of *Don Quixote* and *Sancho Panza* front a stone monument to Cervantes, which was raised in 1927. In *Don Quixote* Cervantes mentions the Leganitos meadow on this site. It acquired a military barracks and became the **Plaza de San Marcial**. In 1931 anti-Church fanatics set fire to the **Convento de Santa Teresa** on the *plaza's* south side. The massive block of the **Edificio España** was completed in 1953 by the Otamendi brothers, an engineer

and an architect, and was an expression of nationalist confidence at a time when Franco's Spain was being ostracised. The **Torre de Madrid**, completed in 1957 in the American mould, was for quite some time the tallest skyscaper in Madrid. The building of the **Real Compañia Asturiana de Minas** displays the admiration for French decoration that was prevalent at the end of the 19th century.
Metro: Plaza de España.

♦♦♦
PLAZA MAYOR
Juan de Herrera, the architect of Felipe II's El Escorial, designed the *plaza's* principal building, the **Casa de la Panadería**, which was completed in 1590. Juan Gómez de Mora was obliged to follow the pattern set by Herrera in completing the building. This was accomplished in 1617 during the reign of Felipe III, whose equestrian statue is in the middle of the *plaza*. Measuring some 394 by 294 feet (120 by 90m), the *plaza* became the capital's grand new venue for executions, *autos-de-fé*, bullfights and other spectacles, which were watched by the court from the balconies of the Casa de la Panadería and by ordinary citizens from balconies on which they had rented space. The *plaza*, pedestrianised in the 1960s and

Plaza Mayor, with its statue of Felipe III, was rebuilt by Juan de Villanueva in 1790

with a parking area below,
remains a popular venue for
cultural events. Bars,
restaurants and some shops
shelter in the surrounding
arcades, and during the warm
months tables and chairs under
bright umbrellas spill out from
them. The Casa de la
Panaderia has been
refurbished to house the
**Centro Cultural Mesonero
Romanos** and other cultural
entities.
Metro: Puerta del Sol, Opera.

◆
PLAZA DE ORIENTE
José Bonaparte ordered the
demolition of existing buildings
and the construction of this
open semi-circle to provide a
better perspective for the

Plaza de la Villa

Palacio Real. The many statues
of royalty were intended for the
balustrade of the palace, but
were found to be too heavy. An
equestrian statue of Felipe IV
was done in 1640 by Pedro de
Tacca, following a painting by
Velázquez.
Metro: Opera.

◆◆◆
PLAZA DE LA VILLA
Medieval, baroque and
Renaissance elements adorn
this handsome small square,
from which Madrid's municipal
affairs are governed. The **Torre
de los Lujanes** dates from the
15th century. Juan Gómez de
Mora designed the **Casa de la
Villa** in 1630, but died before it

was finished in 1695. The use of granite and brickwork, the Flanders-inspired slate roof and the spires are typically his. Juan de Villanueva added the colonnade and balcony facing on to Calle Mayor. The rear façade of the **Casa Cisneros**, also used as municipal offices, was embellished with pieces from various Renaissance buildings in 1910. The main façade of this building, which dates from the early 16th century and is a rare example of Madrid Plateresque architecture, is on Calle Sacramonte.
Open: (Guided tours of some rooms, with notable art) Monday 17.00hrs. *Metro*: Sol, Opera.

PUENTE DE SEGOVIA
The oldest remaining bridge over the meagre Río Manzanares was completed in 1584 by Juan de Herrera, the favourite architect of Felipe II, and shows his typically solid and severe style. The story goes that someone remarked that 'having built a grand bridge, the king would have to buy an appropriate river'.
Metro: La Latina.

◆

PUENTE DE TOLEDO
Felipe V commissioned Pedro de Ribera to design a new bridge across the Río Manzanares to reflect the Bourbon preference for the baroque style. Contrasting greatly with the **Puente de Segovia**, here there are ornamental buttresses and balconies, as well as two small chapels which served as little more than ostentation. Only

three of the nine arches are above water.
Metro: Pirámides.

◆

PUERTA DE ALCALA
Plaza de la Independencia
Like nearby Cibeles, the Puerta de Alcalá is a symbol of the city. Carlos III ordered the construction of a monumental entrance to his city, and it was built in 1778 to the plans of Francisco Sabatini.
Metro: Retiro.

PUERTA DEL SOL
It is not a *puerta* (gateway) to anywhere but an odd-shaped, recently refurbished urban space entered by 10 streets, principally **Calle Alcalá** and **Carrera San Jerónimo** from the east, and **Calles Mayor** and **Arenal** from the west. The name is derived from a figure of *el Sol* (the Sun), which decorated the front of a chapel, since demolished. Where Calle Preciados joins the *Puerta*, is a statue of Madrid's charming emblem, *el osso y madroño*, a bear taking fruit from a strawberry tree. Dominating the south side is what was once the **Casa de Correos** (General Post Office), French architect Jaime Marquet's 1766 example of a late-baroque civic building (the clocktower is an 1866 addition). During Franco's rule it was the headquarters of his feared security services. Now it is used by the Council of Madrid. A slab in its entrance is the zero marking for calculating kilometre distances on Spain's national roads.
Metro: Puerta del Sol.

WHAT TO SEE

◆
SAN FRANCISCO EL GRANDE, REAL BASILICA DE
Plaza San Francisco el Grande
Building was begun in 1761 following the designs of Friar Francisco Cabezas, which bear some resemblance to those of the Pantheon in Rome. The dome is 105 feet (32m) in diameter, larger than London's St Paul's.

Frescoes by Bayeu and others decorate the central cupola and domed chapels. In the first chapel on the left from the entrance is a painting by Goya of Saint Bernardino of Siena.
Metro: La Latina, Puerta de Toledo.

◆◆
TEMPLO DE DEBOD
Ferraz
References and images honouring the god Amón appear in this small temple, which in 1960 was transferred to Madrid from the Nubian Valley, where it would have been submerged by waters of the Aswan Dam. It was given by Egypt to thank Spain for its contribution in saving its monuments. North of here is **La Rosaleda**, a rose garden which is part of the pleasant **Parque del Oeste**.
Open: 10.00–13.00 and 16.00–19.00hrs.
Metro: Plaza de España.

San Francisco el Grande

WALKS IN MADRID

The outlines of three daytime walks are suggested here. Special attention is given to the architectural features of some of the buildings along the routes. Shops, commercial art galleries, places to eat and drink, monuments and everyday street life add to the interest of each walk. Places shown in **bold** type are described more fully in the preceding individual entries. Without allowing for time spent visiting places of interest or for shopping and refreshments, each of the walks will take less than three hours at a gentle pace. If time is very short, the walks can be linked together. Starting early in the morning, walks 1 and 2 can be taken before the *siesta*, and walk 3 can follow a relaxing lunch, perhaps at the legendary Gran Café Gijón. **Plaza de la Cibeles** is the starting point for walk 1, and the finishing point for walk 3. *Metro*: Banco.

◆◆◆
WALK 1: CIBELES TO ORIENTE

From Plaza de la Cibeles go west into Calle de Alcalá. Along on the right are the classical lines of the **Banco Central**, completed in 1918, of which Antonio Palacios was one of the architects. Next on that side, is the **Iglesia de San José**, begun in 1730 and an example of Pedro Ribera's baroque style. On the left at number 42 the **Círculo de Bellas Artes**, designed by Antonio Palacios and completed in 1926, does, as intended, stand out among its surroundings. Further along,

part of the **Ministerio de Educación** is in a small 18th-century palace designed by Juan de Villanueva. Diagonally across from it is the narrow building of the **Dependencias de la Comunidad de Madrid**, completed in 1943, another Antonio Palacios work. Next there is the big dome and the façade (with late-Plateresque elements) of the **Iglesia de las Calatravas**, completed in 1678 and once part of a convent. At number 13 is the **Museo de la Academia de Bellas Artes.** The **Casa Real de Aduana** (number 3), completed in 1769 to a neoclassical design by the Italian Francisco Sabatini, has a soberness which befits its use by the Ministry of Finance. Ahead is the bustling **Puerta del Sol.** On the south side, take Calle Correos and at its end go right into Calle Bolsa to reach **Plaza de la Provincia.** The Ministry of Foreign Affairs occupies the fine **Palacio de Santa Cruz**, completed in 1634 as a court prison and attributed to both Gómez de Mora and the Italian Crescenci. On the right, an archway leads into the **Plaza Mayor.** Exit on the southwest side. Go into Calle Cuchilleros and then right into **Calle Sacramento**, Madrid's most elegant street in the 16th and 17th centuries. On the corner of Calle San Justo is the **Iglesia Pontificia de San Miguel**, a narrow baroque church by the Italian Santiago Bonavia, dating from 1745. Opposite, a lane leads to the **Parroquia de San Andrés y Capilla de San Isidro**. Take Carrera de San Francisco to reach **San**

Francisco el Grande. Go north along Calle de Bailén to cross **El Viaducto**, an impressive piece of urban engineering built between 1934 and 1942. On the corner with Calle Mayor is the **Palacio de Consejos**, now occupied by the military and the state council, a 17th-century work by Juan Gómez de Mora. Continue along Calle Mayor to reach the **Plaza de la Villa.** Next on the right along Calle Mayor is the bright and busy fresh-foods market of **Mercado de San Miguel**. Go left off Calle Mayor into Calle Escalinata in which are the *Murallas Arabes*, the remains of the Arab town's walls. Ahead is the Plaza de Isabel II and the **Teatro Real**, designed by a disciple of Juan de Villanueva

Side-street balconies

and completed in 1850. It reopened in 1992 as the **Teatro de la Opera** after extensive renovation. Continue into the **Plaza de Oriente** where you may want to rest and take refreshment at the **Café de Oriente** before visiting the **Palacio Real** (also known as the Palacio de Oriente).

◆◆◆
WALK 2: ORIENTE TO CIBELES
Linking with Plaza de Oriente and Jardines Cabo Noval is the Plaza de Encarnación with the **Real Monasterio de la Encarnación.** At the end of Calle Encarnación is Plaza de la Marina and at number 2, **La Mi Venta** has a reputation for serving some of the finest *jamón* (bacon) in Madrid; in the winter try its *caldo* (soup). **Palacio de Senado**, seat of the upper house of Spain's parliament, is a neoclassical building from the early 19th century on the site of a former convent. Its modern extension on Calle Bailén was opened in 1991. Ahead is the **Plaza de España**. Go into Calle de Ferraz to the northwest of the *plaza*. First right, on the corner with Calle de Ventura Rodríguez, is the **Museo Cerralbo.** Cross Calle de Ferraz to the **Templo de Debod.** Cross into Calle de Luisa Frenanda and Calle de la Princesa. Cross to the right, passing the entrance to the **Palacio de Liria**, and into Calle de Conde Duque, where a very large former barracks have become the **Centro Cultural del Conde Duque.** Go right into Plaza Cristo and Plaza de Comendadoras. The **Convento**

A LOS HEROES POPULARES QUE EL 2 DE MAYO DE 1808, AUXILIANDO A LOS SOLDADOS DE LOS INMORTALES DAOIZ Y VELARDE, PELEARON AQUI POR LA INDEPENDENCIA DE LA PATRIA CONTRA LAS FUERZAS DE NAPOLEON, EL CIRCULO DE BELLAS ARTES = 1908.

A commemorative plaque in Plaza Dos de Mayo

e Iglesia de las Comendadoras is a large church and convent complex, completed between 1667 and 1753. Along Calle Quiñones is the **Iglesia de Montserrat**, completed in 1704, which has a notable façade by Pedro de Ribera. For a time it served as a women's prison. Across the road, on Calle de San Bernardo, is the **Convento de las Salesas Nuevas**, completed in 1798. At the entrance grille nuns sell biscuits and sweets which they have made. Take Calle de Daoiz to reach **Plaza Dos de Mayo** where the battle against Napoleon's troops is commemorated. Around the square are many bars and eateries. Leave by Calle Velarde and go right into Calle de Fuencarral, to reach the **Museo Municipal.** Next on the left is Calle de San Mateo and the **Museo Romántico**. Go right to cross Calle de Hortaleza and enter Calle Fernando VI. On the

corner with Calle Pelayo, the building of the **Sociedad de Autores** is Madrid's best example of modernist architecture. It bears some resemblance to a Gaudí creation (but is not). Further along the **Iglesia de Santa Bárbara**, completed in the late-18th century, is fully baroque, inside and out. Sabatini designed the tombs of Fernando VI and his wife, Bárbara. The **Palacio de Justicia** (law courts), originally the Salesas Reales Monastery of which the church was part, was rebuilt in 1910 after a fire. Enter **Paseo de Recoletos** with the **Museo Arqueológico** and the **Biblioteca Nacional** opposite, to the left. Down on the right at number 19 is the **Café Gijón** and further along is the **Plaza de la Cibeles**.

◆◆◆
WALK 3: CIBELES

Go south into **Paseo del Prado**. On the left, the **Cuartel General de la Armada** (naval headquarters) and **Museo Naval** incorporate what was the Palacio de Buenavista, begun in 1769, which belonged to the Duquesa de Alba (whom Goya painted). The **Bolsa de Comercio** (stock exchange) is in a neoclassical building dating from the 1880s. The obelisk, rising to 95 feet (29m), was raised in 1840 in honour of the victims of *el Dos de Mayo*. In 1985 it was rededicated as the *Monumento a los Caídos por España*, to honour all who have fallen for Spain. C H Mevves, the French architect also responsible for its sisters in Paris and London, designed the splendid **Hotel Ritz**. Across Calle de Felipe IV, the **Museo Nacional del Prado** forms the first corner of Madrid's glorious 'art triangle'; on the other side of the *paseo*, the Palacio de Villahermosa, housing the **Museo Thyssen-Bornemisza**, forms the second point. Up Calle de Felipe IV and past the **Academia de la Lengua**, guardian of the Castilian language, is the **Casón del Buen Retiro**, long an annexe of the Prado. The building currently housing the **Museo del Ejército** (Army Museum) is also destined for use by the Prado; both buildings are the only remaining parts of the **Palacio de Buen Retiro**, an extensive baroque palace ordered by Felipe IV, which was largely destroyed during the War of Independence. Along Calle Moreto the **Iglesia de San Jerónimo el Real** is a 19th-century reconstruction of a 15th-century church. The **Jardín Botánico** is entered from Plaza de Murillo. From here go left down Paseo del Prado and left again, to see the bookstalls along **Cuesta de Claudio Moyano**. Return to cross **Plaza del Emperador Carlos V**, with its *Fuente de la Alcachofa* (artichoke fountain), into Calle de Santa Isabel to arrive at the third point of the 'art triangle', **Museo Nacional Centro de Arte Reina Sofía**. Estación de Atocha, opposite, is a typical example of late-19th-century iron architecture. On Paseo de la Infanta Isabel, the **Ministerio de Agricultura** is housed in a late-19th-century building by Ricardo Velázquez Bosco, and is also now destined for use by the Museo Nacional del Prado. Two caryatids represent Industry and Commerce while above, Glory is shown giving palms and laurels to Art and Science. Further along is the **Museo Etnológico.** To the right, off Calle de Alfonso XII, is the **Observatorio Astronómico**, a neoclassical concept of Juan de Villanueva, topped by what resembles a small, circular temple. Go along Calle Alfonso XII to enter the delightful **Parque del Retiro**. Leave the park in its northwest corner, where the wide circle of Plaza de la Independencia is graced by the **Puerta de Alcalá**. A short walk to the left brings you to Plaza de la Cibeles.

Parque del Retiro

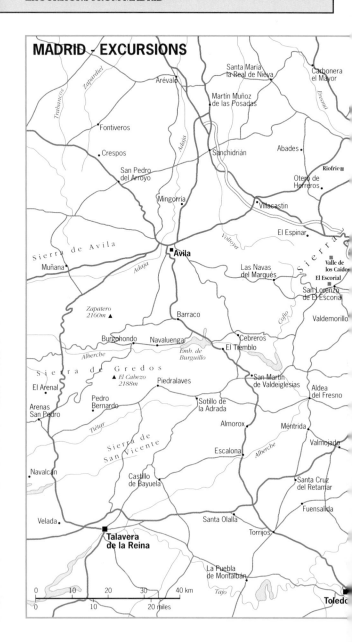

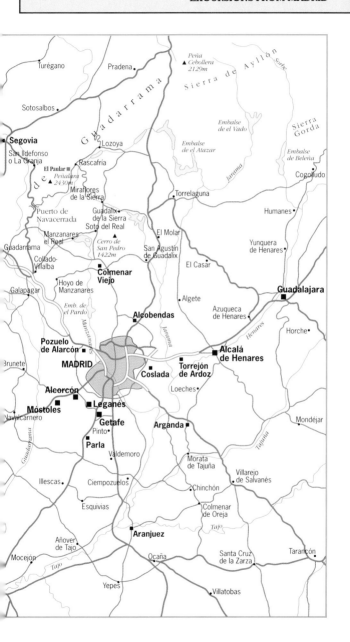

EXCURSIONS FROM MADRID

Within the range of a day excursion from Madrid are many places of interest and beauty, which strongly challenge the capital for rewarding sightseeing. They include a clutch of cities, packed with monumental architecture and loaded with history; grand summer palaces in ordered garden settings, where royalty played and indulged passions for fine decoration; towns and villages which at their core retain storybook images of Castile; imposing castles dominating stretching plains of brown and yellow tones; and green wooded mountains, where streams burble and cosy hamlets nestle. Tree-shaded lakeshores and snowy slopes, with good amenities, await seekers after sports and leisure (see **Sport**). Most conveniently visited on excursions of two or more days, through landscapes in which the spirit of Castilla broods, are beguiling cities like Salamanca and Cuenca.
Details of coach excursions with guides, operated by Juliaturs, Pullmantur and Trapsatur (which are similar in service and prices), are available from local travel agencies and hotel reception desks, which will also make bookings. Renfe runs a number of tourists trains. (For further information, tel: 733 1629.) Its *Tren de la Fresa* (Strawberry Train) is very popular. It has a steam engine and wooden carriages, and goes on day excursions to Aranjuez (see page 56) on Saturdays, Sundays and public holidays from May to October, along Spain's second-oldest rail route. Attendants in period costume serve strawberries, and a brass band plays a welcome.
Regular train and bus services are convenient for lower-cost, more flexible independent arrangements. With your own or a hired vehicle there is even more opportunity to go where and when you please. Outlines of a selection of excursion destinations follow; firstly those within the Council of Madrid, and then the three capitals of adjoining provinces.

◆◆
ALCALA DE HENARES
20 miles (30km) east of Madrid
Alcalá, on the Río Henares, was the site of an Iberian settlement which became the Roman *villa* of *Complutum*. Today industrial sprawl hides the monumental centre of a town with strong literary and academic associations. In 1492, the year that Colón (Columbus) reached the Americas, Antonio de Nebrija published the first Castilian grammar compendium in Alcalá. Six years later Cardenal Cisneros, the clerical strongman of *los Reyes Católicos*, founded the Complutense university and by 1517 ordered the publication of the famous *Biblia Políglota Complutense* (Complutensian Polyglot Bible), one of the most celebrated versions of the Bible in a number of ancient languages. In 1547 Miguel de Cervantes y Saavedra, the greatest *maestro* of Spanish

literature, was born in the town, where his life and times are worshipfully evoked in the reconstructed **Casa de Cervantes** on Calle de la Imagen.

Most imposing of the town's numerous notable buildings is the University, whose main façade perfectly expresses the Plateresque style. Beyond it lie cloisters and patios of impeccable proportions and adornment. Adjoining the University is its original chapel, the **Iglesia de San Ildefonso**, Gothic in design and Plateresque in embellishment, as well as the **Colegio de San Pedro y San Pablo**. Spread around are other college buildings, which remained in use until the university was transferred to Madrid in 1837. Not to be missed among the many religious buildings are: the **Palacio Arzobispal**, started

Alcalá de Henares' university is its pride

in the 13th century and showing a harmony of styles – Mudéjar, Byzantine, Gothic and Renaissance; the austerely elegant **Iglesia Magistral**, begun in 1136 but principally Gothic, whose tower dominates the town and contains the tomb of Cardenal Cisneros and the image of Alcalá's patroness, Nuestra Señora de Val; and the brick-built **Ermita de la Virgen del Val**, which shows the Gothic-Mudéjar style.

Notable in the **Convento de la Imagen**, where the sister of Cervantes was once prioress, are stairs and balustrades of wrought stone, while Juan Gómez de Mora, the leading architect of Habsburg Madrid, designed the **Monasterio de las Bernardas**, distinguished for its nave and elliptical cupola.

Charitable institutions, too, raised fine buildings in the town, among them the Hospital de Antezana and Hospital de Estudiantes.

Restaurant
The **Hosteria del Estudiantes** (tel: 888 0330) in the *Paraninfo* (Great Hall) of the University, can be highly recommended for its ambience and traditional dishes.

◆◆
ARANJUEZ
29 miles (47km) south of Madrid
At the confluence of the Rios Tajo and Jarama is a green oasis which has been treasured since Neolithic times. Its productiveness was most expertly exploited during the Arab occupation. Today, strawberries and asparagus are its most acclaimed produce. In the Middle Ages it was the domain of the military order of Santiago, which was dispossessed of its privilege by *los Reyes Católicos*. Under Felipe II the Grand Master's palace on the banks of the Tajo was transformed into a grander construction, largely destroyed by fires in the 1660s.
In 1715, Felipe V ordered the reconstruction and enlargement of a new **Palacio Real**, (continued by his successors until 1839), and different architects managed to create a harmonious whole. Carlos III gave impetus to developing the extensive and delightful gardens shaded by tall plane and mighty elm trees with ornamental areas graced by statuary and fountains celebrating different themes and styles. In the Jardín del

Fountains abound in the gardens of Palacio Real, Aranjuez

Príncipe, the largest and most beautiful area, is the **Casa del Labrador**, a neoclassical palace of the Bourbon court, erected at the end of the 18th century in emulation of the Petit Trianon at Versailles.

Today, rooms with silk-lined walls in various styles have rich displays of furniture, clocks, statues and ceramics. These things, and more, are also to be seen on conducted tours through the **Palacio Real**. Many paintings adorn the grand rooms, but most are copies of works to be seen in the Prado or other collections. Outstanding among the sumptuous rooms are the **Salón de Porcelana**, decorated with fine 18th-century pieces from Madrid's Buen Retiro porcelain factory, and **La Capilla**, which Sabatini designed and Bayeu decorated. Access to the Palacio Real is across a 25-arch stone bridge, constructed in 1761. During the reign of Fernando VI, Aranjuez ceased to be the preserve of royalty, and noble families built summer homes there. Gradually a town (now of limited attraction for visitors) developed.

Restaurant
La Rana Verde, Calle Reina 1 (tel: 891 1325), with its terrace facing the palace gardens and diningroom overlooking the Tajo, is a good place for local fare.

◆
COLMENAR DE OREJA Y CHINCHON
Fourteen miles (22km) northeast of Aranjuez, is **Colmenar de Oreja**, a typical Castilian *pueblo* with a galleried *plaza* of the style which was adopted in the Americas. Notable, too, are its parish church, the Convento de Agustinas Descalzas, Ermita del Cristo del Humilladero and the Museo de Ulpiano Checa, displaying works of the locally born painter (1860–1916). Winemaking is a growing industry.

Three miles (5km) further north is **Chinchón,** which merits a visit for its picturesque Plaza Mayor.This is of irregular shape and lined by houses with wooden balconies, used by spectators to watch bullfights and other spectacles. Within the tall Iglesia de la Asunción (a mixture of Gothic, Renaissance and baroque styles), is a painting by Goya, whose brother, Camilo, served here as a priest. Other notable buildings are the Convento de Santa Clara and the Casa de la Cadena. On the outskirts are the remains of 15th-century **Castillo de los Condes de Chinchón**. The town is famous for its production of *aguardientes* (liqueurs), and for attractive ceramics: both good mementoes of a visit.

Restaurants
Classic Castilian cuisine at honest prices can be enjoyed on the plaza at the **Mesón de la Virreina** (tel: 894 0015). The 18th-century Monasterio de los Agustinos has been converted into the **Parador del Turismo** (tel: 894 0836), highly recommended for its lodging and restaurant.

◆◆◆
EL ESCORIAL

31 miles (50km) northwest of Madrid

Felipe II, that powerful monarch of sober countenance, gave great consideration to the choice of location for his monastery, palace and royal pantheon. They were to have a grandeur commensurate with Spain's greatness during the 16th century. Felipe chose a wooded site 3,370 feet (1,028m) above sea level, in the foothills of the Sierra de Guadarrama. Juan Bautista de Toledo began the project in 1563 and, after his death four years later, he was succeeded by Juan de Herrera, who completed the work in 1584. The king's two favourite architects achieved an austere and brooding pile of grey granite, which matched Felipe's sombre disposition. The dimensions of the rectangular mass of this, Spain's largest building, are awesome: 680 by 530 feet (207 by 161m) in total, with corner towers rising to 180 feet (55m). The two campaniles reach 236 feet (72m), while the cupola of the basilica is closer to heaven, at just over 300 feet (92m). The construction is just as staggering, with 300 rooms, 15 cloisters, 16 patios, 88 fountains, more than 1,500 doors and 2,600 windows. Today, parts of the complex are still used as a college and monastery. Guides shepherd visitors through parts of principal interest. The large **Patio de los Reyes** is named after the six kings of Israel, who are represented in statues on the front of the basilica, the centrepiece of the grandiose complex. Guides give detailed descriptions of the decoration within, which includes the **Capilla Mayor** and **Tabernáculo** by Juan de Herrera, and bronzes by Pompeyo Leoni of Carlos V, Felipe II and their wives. Since Carlos V all monarchs of Spain have been entombed in the marble niches of the **Panteón de Reyes**, a work by Juan Gómez de Mora and Juan Bautista Crescenci, completed in 1645. The monastery's **Sacristía** has paintings by Spanish, Italian and Flemish artists; *La Sagrada Forma*, an acclaimed work by

Claudio Coello, dominates over an altar. More paintings adorn other cloisters and gallery rooms. Frescoes, mainly by Italian artists, decorate the two high **Salas Capitulares**. The finest work is in the **Museo de Pinturas**, which includes works by Ribera, Velázquez, Valdés Leal and Alonso Cano. Murals depicting battles won by Spain cover the huge **Sala de Batallas**, while precious codices, manuscripts and books are treasured in the imposing **Bibliotecas's** extensive collection. Virtually unchanged since the time of Felipe II are the austere rooms within the **Palacio de los Austrias** (Habsburgs). From his bare quarters here the king could watch the celebration of Mass in the basilica, and here he died, after becoming increasingly reclusive as his empire weakened.

By contrast, the **Palacio de los Borbones**, in whose design Juan de Villanueva collaborated, has an elaborate decoration in Pompeiian style, with rich furnishings and tapestries designed by Goya. Within the estate grounds are two pleasure pavilions by Juan de Villanueva – the **Casita del Príncipe** and the **Casita del**

Imposing El Escorial

Infante (Arriba) – which display the Bourbon taste for rich decoration.

The village of **San Lorenzo del Escorial** is a favoured summer resort of *Madrileños*. Eight miles (13km) north is **El Valle de los Caídos** (The Valley of the Fallen) Franco's new name for the lovely Valle de Cuelgamuros, in which he commemorated victims of the Civil War. Political prisoners toiled to tunnel a basilica in the granite hill of Nava, and to raise a gigantic cross atop it, some 500 feet (152m) tall and 140 feet (43m) wide. Below the eerie basilica's mosaic-covered cupola are the tombs of the dictator and his more benevolent predecessor, José Antonio Primo de Rivera.

Restaurants
Charoles, Calle Floridablanca 24 (tel: 890 5975), has terraces as well as cosily rustic diningrooms, and offers high-style Spanish cooking. It is a top restaurant. Simpler and cheaper is **La Cueva**, Calle San Antón 4 (tel: 890 1516).

◆◆
AVILA
69 miles (110km) northwest of Madrid
Spain's highest provincial capital lies 3,700 feet (1,128m)

Rooftops in Avila

above sea level, on a spur overlooking the Río Adaja and a boulder-strewn plain, with the Sierra de Avila as a backdrop. Europe's best preserved medieval town walls, *Las Murallas,* first completed in 1099, still surround the city. Their design is unique in Spain, notable for many *cubos* (cylindrical towers), 88 in all, and nine gates (formed by two towers connected by an arch). On the east side (where defences were most vulnerable owing to the flatness of the land), are the two strongest gates, San Vicente and Alcázar. Here too is the fortified apse of the **Catedral**, dating from the same period, which projects into the walls. The cathedral is mainly Gothic, but contains elements of Romanesque and baroque styles. The Romanesque **Basílica de San Vicente**, just outside the gate, is built on the site of the martyrdom of the saint and his two sisters in AD303. A wander through Avila's streets reveals that it is packed with noble houses, churches and convents. Notable is the Gothic **Convento de Santo Tomás,** ordered by *los Reyes Católicos,* and in which their only son, Juan, and Inquisitor, Torquemada, are buried. Apart from its walls Avila is famed as the birthplace of Santa Teresa (1515–82), a girl of noble birth who became a nun at the **Convento de la Concepción** when she was 18. She later gained great veneration and influence through her mystical visions and writings, and reformed the Carmelite order. One of its many convents is the baroque **Convento de Santa Teresa,** built on the site of her birthplace. Mementoes of the saint are big business in Avila; for instance *yemas de Santa Teresa* (sweets made with egg yolks), are a local delicacy.

Restaurants

The **Parador de Turismo** (tel: (918) 211 340), in a 15th-century palace abutting the city walls, is an enchanting place to sample local cooking, while **El Molina de la Losa** (tel: (918) 211 101), is a converted 15th-century water mill next to the Puente de Adaja. Good Castilian cooking is offered on terraces with views of the city walls.

SEGOVIA

53 miles (85km) northwest of Madrid

This charming city – dreamily evocative of the past, and lively in the present – is raised on a spur between two rivers. From afar its many towers, turrets and domes soar high above the Castilian plain. At the prow of the spur is the **Alcázar,** which gained its fairytale look in an 1880s remodelling. A fortress built on the site during the 12th century grew in size and importance, and in 1474 Isabel I was crowned queen of Castile here. Some original rooms remain, recalling the period when Avila was one of Spain's most influential cities. The huge yet graceful **Catedral**, begun in 1525, was the last major Gothic construction undertaken in Spain. Its tall, light interior is sparsely decorated, and

peaceful adjoining cloisters remain from an earlier cathedral destroyed by fire.

The oldest and most exceptional of Segovia's grand monuments is the **Acueducto Romano** built in the 1st century AD in local granite, without mortar or cement. It is among the finest examples of its kind still existing. Supported by 167 arches, it runs some 2,390 feet (728m), and rises 95 feet (29m) high above the Plaza del Azoguejo. Within the old town's robust walls are narrow *calles* and pretty *plazas*, like Conde de Cheste, San Martín and the café-lined Plaza Mayor. Numerous Romanesque churches with rounded apses and square belfries are distinguished in Segovia by their covered porticoes, where artisans and traders once gathered. Principal examples are San Esteban, San Martín, San Juan de los Caballeros, Iglesia de la Trinidad and, beyond the walls, San Millán and San Lorenzo.

Many of the town's noble houses have *esgrafiado*, a stuccowork decoration. Below the north walls is the **Iglesia de la Vera Cruz,** built in its twelve-sided shape in the 13th century by the Knights Templar. From its belltower there is a good view of the city and the Alcázar. Nearby is the **Monasterio del Parral**, founded in 1459, one of the most interesting monasteries of the town, in a lovely setting. The small town of **La Granja de San Ildefonso**, seven miles (11km) southeast

Segovia's Alcázar

of Segovia, has a royal palace ordered by Felipe V in imitation of Versailles, where he spent his youth. The decorations and furnishings, in French Imperial style, are mostly of Spanish manufacture, including the chandeliers and mirrors made at the local *Fabrica de Cristales* (glassworks). The estate has woodlands and a formal garden, with impressive fountains, one 130 feet (80m) high.

Restaurants

Segovia is considered the custodian of traditional Castilian cuisine, and the atmospheric **Mesón de Cándido**, Plaza Azoguejo 5 (tel: (911) 425 911), is almost a national institution. Cheaper, with simple meals and a pleasant *plaza* is **Narizotas**, Medina del Campo 2 (tel: (911) 431 806).

◆◆◆
TOLEDO
44 miles (70km) southwest of Madrid

Declared a national monument in its entirety, the city of Toledo ranks high as one of Europe's most visited sites, but its magnificence is somewhat spoiled by the tourist trade's tattiness. Off season, or early in the morning and late in the afternoon, when the crowds are thin, is the best time to discover this rich and varied architectural assembly, resonant with Spanish history. Imposingly sited and surrounded on three sides by the gorge of the Río Tajo, Toledo has witnessed the knotting of successive strands which have formed Spanish

EXCURSIONS FROM MADRID

civilisation. By the close of the 2nd century, the Romans were building their town, *Toletum*, on what had been a Celtiberian settlement. In the 6th century it became the capital from which the Visigoths ruled Spain, and Arabs replaced them in 712. Alfonso VI, with the help of *El Cid*, captured Toledo in 1085, making it the capital of Christian Castile. The town had prospered under Arab rule, when Jews and Christians were allowed to retain their religions and cultures, and its population exceeded 200,000. Craft and art talents were encouraged, and Toledo's scholars spread scientific knowledge and philosophy from Classical, Arab and Jewish cultures to Dark Age Europe. Under the rule of Castile these trends continued and Alfonso X, The Wise (1217–1284), was especially eager to promote the productive fusion of cultures. By the time of *los Reyes Católicos,* attitudes had changed and the Inquisition's persecution of Muslims and Jews caused a great number of accomplished people to leave Toledo. During the 16th century the town was briefly the capital of united Spain, until Felipe II passed the honour to Madrid. Toledo retained the see of Spain's Catholic Primate, however.

Now, as in those days, the triangular **Plaza del Zocodover** (Arabic for market), is the city's bustling focal point and the best place to begin an exploration on foot. Surrounding buildings hide the full majesty of the **Catedral**, which was started in

the 13th century and completed some 200 years later. Beyond the Puerta de Mollete, and through the cloister, is the huge interior, an overwhelming mixture of Gothic, Renaissance and baroque styles, with decorative sculpture in wood and stone, and with frescoes and paintings, stained glass and intricate wrought iron. Finely carved scenes from the conquest of Granada cover the choir stalls, while New Testament tales are told on the tall altarpiece. Most fanciful of all is the *Transparente*, a naturally lit, baroque configuration combining painting and sculpture. Mass is conducted daily in a chapel below the cupola. Among the Catedral's prized possessions is a silver and gilt monstrance, weighing some 400 pounds (180kg). A fine carved ceiling graces the Sala Capitular, and in the Sacristía's (Sacristry's) fine art collection are works by El Greco, Velázquez and Goya. El Greco's son contributed to the fine-looking **Ayuntamiento** building.

Southwest from here is the **Judería**, the old Jewish quarter, which is full of places of interest. The **Palacio de Fuensalida,** a restored 15th-century palace, adjoins the **Taller de Moro,** where artisans employed on the cathedral once worked, and which has examples of their workmanship. Within the **Iglesia de Santo Tomé** is one of El Greco's most acclaimed paintings, *Entierro del Conde de Orgaz*. A 16th-century house was rebuilt in the

town to become the **Casa del Greco** which, together with an adjoining museum, now displays some of the artist's notable paintings. A financier and adviser to the king, Samuel Levy, had the **Sinagoga del Tránsito** built in the 1360s. It is now home to a Sephardic Museum. An older, 13th-century building is the tiny, white and beautiful **Santa María la Blanca,** originally a synagogue. To celebrate their victory over the Portuguese in 1476, *los Reyes Católicos* ordered the building of the **Monasterio de San Juan de los Reyes,** which exemplifies the Gothic style of that period and has a fine cloister.
A Visigoth museum is to be found in the 13th-century **Iglesia de San Román**, and the **Puerta del Sol** gatehouse affords good views across the

Historic Toledo

town and beyond. Close to it is **Cristo de la Luz**, a small 11th-century mosque, one of Spain's best examples of early Moorish architecture. The original Plateresque façade of the **Hospital de Santa Cruz**, completed in 1515, was damaged during the Civil War. It conceals spacious halls, grand staircases, elaborate ceilings and a lovely patio, as well as the varied collection of the Museo Provincial.
A Roman fort, Visgothic citadel and Arab *alcázar* all once stood on the site of Carlos V's fortress palace. Of uncompromising bulk, it is still called the **Alcázar.** It has been much restored over the centuries, most recently after a siege in the Civil War, which diehard Francoists still recall with pride.

EXCURSIONS FROM MADRID

Outside the city walls are two medieval bridges, the **Puente San Martín** and the **Puente de Alcántara**. The **Hospital de Tavera**, a charitable foundation of the 16th century, displays period furniture and art, including a number of El Grecos.

Restaurants
Plenty of places offer *menus del día,* although some are tourist traps. **Asador Adolfo**, Calle La Granada 6 (tel: (925) 227 321) provides a memorable experience of modern Spanish cooking in a 14th-century house. Simpler local dishes at fair prices can be enjoyed in the modern atmosphere of **La Tarasca**, Calle Hombre de Palo 6 (tel: (925) 224 342).

Toledo's 400-year-old Puerta del Cambrón

Peace and Quiet

Wildlife and Countryside in and around Madrid
By Paul Sterry

Much to the surprise of many first-time visitors inland Spain is full of extraordinary and dramatic contrasts: typically Mediterranean landscapes in the lowlands give way to vast stretches of arid semi-deserts, and eroded sandstone gorges rise through forested slopes to rugged mountains and snow-capped peaks. Almost all these strikingly different habitats could, conceivably, be seen in a single day's drive from Madrid.

Birdwatchers, in particular, will find that Madrid is a superb base from which to search for some of Spain's most exciting species. Many of the good areas can be visited on day trips from the city, while overnight stops may be a preferred option for other regions. The mountains to the north and west of Madrid are home to a wealth of birds of prey, while the plains have open-country species such as bustards, larks and sandgrouse.

Most of the floral interest of the region is found in the mountains. Here, alpine plants can be seen growing alongside many endemic flowers such as tulips and daffodils. Add to these natural history treasures the superb scenery of central Spain and most visitors with an interest in wildlife will be enthralled. A word of warning, however: many of the sites within a day's journey of Madrid are extremely popular with the city's residents. Weekends and public holidays can make some of the narrow mountain roads extremely busy. Try to visit potentially popular spots on week days.

Sierra de Gredos

The Sierra de Gredos is a vast range of mountains which runs west from Madrid towards the border with Portugal. The focal point of the range is Arenas de San Pedro, approximately 80 miles (130km) west of Madrid. Take the M501 and C501 via San Martin de Valdeiglesias and Piedralaves to Arenas. Alternatively, take the N502 from Avila via Ouerto del Pico. The area to the north and west of Arenas de San Pedro comprises the Reserva Nacional de Gredos.

PEACE AND QUIET

The Sierra de Gredos rise to 8,504 feet (2,592m) at the highest point, Pico Almanzor. The southern slopes of the range have a Mediterranean feel, with maquis flowers such as tree heathers and cistuses and trees including olive and holm oak. The northern slopes, on the other hand, do not receive the same warming influence and have alpine pines and plants.

There are hotels in Arenas as well as in many of the villages to the north and west of the town, on the slopes of the Sierra de Gredos. The countryside can be explored both from the roads through the region and from villages in the Sierra. There are particularly fine views and vantage points on the loop roads from Arenas via Guisando and El Arenal. The Sierra de Gredos is superb for birds of prey: it is worth spending time scanning the skies from a vantage point overlooking a valley or close to a series of peaks. Mornings are generally best for observing them as they take to the wing, riding the thermals generated by the warming slopes. In a short time, you could see kites, eagles, buzzards and vultures, often in considerable numbers.

Sierra de Guadarrama, a haven for wildlife

Black Vultures

The black vulture is Europe's largest vulture and also perhaps the rarest. One of its last strongholds is in the mountains around Madrid, where it can still be seen in good numbers. Their broad wings enable them to soar with ease, as they scan the ground below for carrion such as dead mammals. They have suffered from persecution in the past but are now fully protected; however, another factor in their decline is that nowadays there is less carrion on the mountain slopes for them to feed on.

Sierra de Guadarrama

This mountain range lies northwest of Madrid – its nearest slopes are less than 35 miles (60km) from the city. The sierras are something of a playground for Madrid's residents, but the wildlife is nevertheless abundant and varied and peace and quiet can easily be found.

A good base from which to explore the area is Miraflores, reached by taking the E5 north from Madrid and turning off on the M608 after roughly 28 miles (45km). Alternatively, take the M607 northwards from the city and turn off on the M611 after about 18 miles (30km). For most people, the best way to explore the Sierra de Guadarrama on a short visit is to drive the mountain roads, making frequent stops to admire the views and study the wildlife.

If staying at Miraflores, take the M611 over the sierra. Search the lower woodlands for birds such as azure-winged magpies and the high passes for alpine species of bird and flower. On sunny days, vultures – mostly griffon vultures – can be seen everywhere in the skies. On one day in April, I stopped counting when I got to 200 in the air at once! Another good road is the one to Segovia via Puerto de Navacerrada. Stop at Puerto de Navacerrada and walk west on the track to Siete Picos.

Wildlife interest is not confined to birds by any means. In the open woodland on the southern slopes, look for green-winged orchids, tulips, tree heathers and bluebells. Higher up you will find hoop daffodils and crocuses often growing close to the road. Eyed lizards bask on the granite outcrops and butterflies are numerous and varied.

Parque Regional de la Cuenca Alta del Manzanares

The park lies on the northwest fringes of Madrid and, not surprisingly, is extremely popular at weekends and holidays. Within the park's boundaries is dramatic limestone scenery, made easily accessible by a network of walks and trails. To reach the park, drive north from Madrid on the M607 which goes to Manzanares.

Just after Colmenar Viejo, roughly 18 miles (30km) from

PEACE AND QUIET

the city, turn off left to the park entrance. Look for vultures and other birds of prey soaring overhead and lizards basking on the rocks.

Eyed Lizard

A full-grown eyed lizard is the largest lizard found on the Iberian peninsula. Large specimens may exceed 3 feet (1m) in length, and have bulky bodies. Their diet comprises mainly insects and other invertebrates, although they will tackle any suitably sized animal they can catch, including small mammals, birds and even other lizards. Eyed lizards are beautifully marked, their colouration gradually changing as they grow. The background colour is a variable shade of green and eye markings are often prominent on the body.

Kestrels are often seen

Birds of Open Country and Agricultural Land

A surprising variety of birds can be seen while driving along backroads on the outskirts of Madrid – many of these are open country species that have adapted to the change in land use to cereal production. Minor roads to the east of Madrid, between the E90 at Guadalajara and the E5 which runs north to Aranda de Duero, can be good. Bee-eaters are a common sight during the summer months. Their plumage is a mixture of almost every colour and they excavate nest holes in sandy banks beside the roads. Birds of prey such as kestrels and Montagu's harriers are often seen, but pride of place must go to the great bustards. These are Europe's largest birds and among the largest in the world still capable of flight. They are rather shy, but small flocks are sometimes seen flying overhead as they move from one field to another.

Serrania de Cuenca

This mountain range lies east of Madrid and rises to over 5,250 feet (1,600m) in places. It is best explored from Cuenca, 100 miles (160km) from the city. Take the E901 southeast from Madrid to Tarancon and then the N400 east to Cuenca. From the town, numerous minor roads lead up into the mountain, for example to La Toba and La Ciudad Encantada.

The landscape of the Serrania de Cuenca is varied – eroded limestone (most notably perhaps at La Ciudad Encantada) gorges, woodland and open mountain tops. Lime-loving plants, including many orchids, are abundant and varied in the spring and the identification of birds of prey provides a challenge.

The northeastern flank of the range harbours the Reserva Nacional de la Serrania de Cuenca. This is crossed by the

The green-winged orchid, one of 20 species found in central Spain

minor road from Villalba de la Sierra to Alto de la Vega at 4,888 feet (1,490m). Nearby to the west is the Reserva Nacional de los Montes Universales, which can be explored on roads from Albarracin or Guadalaviar.

Parque Natural del Alto Tajo

This park lies 95 miles (150km) east of Madrid and protects the upper reaches of the River Tagus. The scenery is spectacular, with dramatic, eroded gorges and raging river torrents. Take the E90 northeast from Madrid, through Guadalajara as far as the junction with the N211.

Orchids

In spring, sunny slopes and woodland clearings in central Spain become covered in colourful flowers. One of the most exciting groups to be found here is the orchids – more than 20 species could be considered common and widespread around Madrid, most doing particularly well where the underlying rock is limestone. Most orchids have unusually shaped flowers, many of which have evolved to attract specific insects for pollination. The bee orchid family is especially bizarre in appearance and has names such as bumblebee, wasp, woodcock and sawfly orchid. A group of orchids known as helleborines also do well on sunny slopes in Spain, especially in woodland clearings. The red helleborine is perhaps the most attractive of these, despite the fact that it usually only has four or five flowers on a flower spike.

PEACE AND QUIET

Take this road to Molina de Aragón and just before the town turn right on the GU914 into the park. Where the road crosses the Tagus, turn southeast and follow the road which runs parallel with the river.

Laguna de Gallocanta

Although this site lies roughly 125 miles (200km) from Madrid, it is well worth the effort required to get there if you are a keen birdwatcher. Not only do the reedbeds and marshes of the lake harbour vast numbers of waterbirds both in summer and winter, but the surrounding arid semi-desert is home to exciting and otherwise elusive species. To reach Laguna de Gallocanta, drive northeast from Madrid on through Guadalajara and take the N211 as far as Molina de Aragón. Turn off on the C211 towards Daroca and drive for about 25 miles (40km).

The arid country that you cross between Molina de Aragón and Laguna de Gallocanta is superb for birds. Griffon vultures are often in the skies and several species of larks can be seen. Sandgrouse, little bustards and great grey shrikes also find this habitat much to their liking.

The shores of the lake are best viewed by exploring minor farm tracks from the villages of Gallocanta, Berrueco, Tornos or Bello. Ducks, herons, egrets and terns are here in spring and summer, while in winter, hundreds of cranes arrive from northern Europe. Nearby, the Laguna de Zaida can be viewed from tracks off the C211.

The crested lark

Practical

This section (with the yellow band) includes food, drink, shopping, accommodation, nightlife, tight budget, special events etc

FOOD AND DRINK

Although Madrid is relatively far from the sea, it is one of the best places in Europe to partake of a wide selection of fresh seafood. It has long been (and remains) a central concern of Spain's fishing industry to satisfy the discriminating tastes of the capital's inhabitants, who are prepared to pay well for quality and freshness. All types of Spanish cuisine can be sampled in Madrid, but foreigners may be unaware of the diversity of Spain's regional cuisines. Those of *País Vasco* (the Basque country) and *Catalunya* (Catalonia) are the most highly rated; in them, great care is taken with sauces, and the combination of ingredients is subtle. The more refined cooking of both areas reflects the fact that they are still Spain's most economically successful regions. The cuisines of other regions should certainly not be ignored, though. For instance, *paella* originates from the Valencia region, and *gazpacho*, that delicious and refreshing cold soup, is a staple of Andalucía.

The foods of many other countries are becoming increasingly common in Madrid – from the most exotic dishes to Big Macs. Vegetarians and health-food fans need not fear, as these days there are plenty of restaurants catering for them.

The Food and Drink Schedule

Foreigners often remark that the *Madrileños'* attention seems to be concentrated on the (almost continuous) consumption of food and drink, in hearty quantities. They have been observing locals when they are out and about in bars and restaurants, perhaps for some celebration, or while on business. They have not observed the *Madrileños'* more modest consumption of food at home. In a hotel, for instance, a traditional breakfast starts with coffee or a creamy chocolate drink, with either toast, a croissant or *churros* (strips of deep-fried batter, dipped in caster sugar). It is no disgrace also to take a shot of alcohol, like a *coñac* (brandy) or a *sol y sombra*, a 'sun-and-shade' mix of aniseed and brandy. Later in

FOOD AND DRINK

the morning a snack is taken: often a *tostada* (toasted sandwich), with something to drink which, if it has to be alcoholic, is usually a *cerveza* (beer). The ritual is to take an *aperitivo* or two with some *tapas* (snacks) before *almuerzo* (lunch), the big meal of the day which starts after 14.00hrs and

can be accompanied by bacchanalian imbibings. Around 18.00hrs a *merienda* (snack) is taken – more coffee and pastries. After work (if any has really been done since lunch), it is time for more *aperitivos* and *tapas*. The evening meal at home is light, and taken after 22.00hrs. Around this time the restaurants start to fill up with people

A typical tapas bar

Tapas – A Healthy Habit

Tapas is derived from *tapar* (to cover). Traditionally in Andalucia, glasses were covered with a small plate, and it became the custom to put a free snack on it. *Aceitunas* (olives) and *nueces* (nuts) are the simplest snacks, usually served free with beer, wine or sherry. But *tapas* can be small portions of almost any type of food, in a variety of preparations, simple or elaborate. They are usually displayed on a counter and you order, and pay for, what you want. *Tapas* can be a good way of trying out several local food specialities, without straining your budget or your digestion. Eating while drinking alcohol certainly has the effect of slowing down the drinking rate (because you have something else to do with your hands and mouth), and of countering the intoxicating effects of the drinks. For this reason it is rare to see reelingly drunk Spaniards, in spite of a generally high level of alcohol consumption.

wanting *cena* (dinner). They may be the same people who have followed the day's ingestion routine fully, and this dinner will be a three-course affair, with a steady intake of wine, followed by brandy or a liqueur of some sort.

Three factors are having an effect on traditional eating and drinking nowadays. In a high-pressure, competitive world, Madrid's decision-makers cannot afford to spend much of their afternoons over lunch, sitting for the rest of the working day in a half-dazed frame of mind. There is also a greater awareness of health and beauty, especially among the young and better-educated. Finally, bar and restaurant prices have risen sharply.

Local Foods and Dishes

For a full experience of local foods and dishes, the following should not be missed. *Churros con chocolate*; the choice for beginning the day. As a starter to a main meal order *sopa de ajo* or *sopa castellana,* garlic soup with paprika, bread, ham and egg. Another choice could be *potaje de garbanzos y espinacas,* chick pea and spinach soup. If you want to order the 'national' dish, *cocido madrileño,* be prepared for a ceremony as much as a gargantuan meal, for this boiled stew comes in three servings: firstly, the broth, to which a thin pasta has been added; next, the vegetables, which include chick peas, carrots, turnips, celery, onions, potatoes and cabbage; and lastly, the meat – beef, chicken, veal, pork, ham bone

and *chorizo* (a paprika-spiced sausage). Some people who have unwittingly ordered another local favourite, *callos a la madrileña,* have had to rush from the table in disgust: it is tripe with *chorizo* and *morcilla* (blood sausage) in a long-cooked and tasty stew with peppers, tomatoes, onions and spices. Safer bets are *lombarda de San Isidro,* a red cabbage, potato and wine vinegar stew, or *judias blancas a lo tío Lucas,* a preparation of haricot beans, named after Uncle Lucas, a local chef. Or try *bacalao al ajo arriero,* a Castilian preparation of cod with garlic, and *besugo al horno,* baked sea bream. Castilla is a meat-producing region; lamb and pork are plentiful. The preference is to savour the meat of very young animals, either simply roasted in wood-fired *asadores* (ovens), or cooked on a spit so that it is crispy on the outside and juicy inside. *Cochinillo asado* or *el tostón* is roast suckling pig; *cordero asado* roast lamb. Both are memorable gastronomic experiences which meat-eaters should not miss. For dessert, try the simple *flan,* a crème caramel, or *leche frita,* a square of creamy fried custard with a crunchy crust. *Queso manchego,* sheep's milk cheese from the Castilla-La Mancha region, is Spain's top-rated cheese. As a dessert, it is often served with honey or quince jelly.

Wine

Anyone with a serious interest in this subject should buy a current guide to Spanish wines.

FOOD AND DRINK

The country is one of the world's major producers, with a fascinating diversity from different *Denominaciones de Origen* or DOs, demarcated wine-growing areas subject to strict quality controls. Best known in export markets are those from Rioja and Penedés. La Mancha, the DO south of Madrid, which produces around a third of the national wine total, is not renowned for quality, but within it can be found some treasures, like Estola. Vega Sicilia, the most expensive Spanish vintage wine, is from Ribera del Duero, north of Madrid; Valbuena is an earlier bottling of the same fine wine. High-tech *bodegas* in the DO of Rueda have recently been creating surprises with their new wines. The Catalan DO of Penedés also produces *cava*, a sparkling wine made by the champagne method which out-sells French champagne in the United States. The best quality cava is *brut* and *brut nature*, both excellent value for money.

Besides relying on the advice of the waiter or *sommelier* (which can be bad news in unscrupulous places), the easiest option is to order *vino de la casa* (house wine) – either *tinto* (red), *blanco* (white) or *rosado* (rosé). In most places in Madrid these wines will come from the DOs of La Mancha or Valdepeñas. Regional restaurants tend to feature wines from their local DOs. For example, Galician restaurants will serve Ribeiro, and in Valencian establishments there is most likely to be Jumilla wine.

The Bear and the Berry Tree
The coat-of-arms of the Villa de Madrid shows a bear picking berries from a *madroño* (strawberry tree), and on the Puerta del Sol a bronze sculpture repeats the scene. The fruit – red outside and yellow inside – is used to make one of the city's favourite liqueurs, simply called *madroño*. It is another of Madrid's taste experiences and, without more description, visitors can have a little surprise in store.

Other Drinks

Alcoholic

Think of a drink and you can get it in Madrid, either made in Spain or imported, and in measures larger than you may be used to. That is a warning! Foreigners accustomed to smaller measures and more restricted licensing hours can easily over-indulge. The strength of ordinary Spanish beer (*cerveza*) is between 4.6

and 5.4 per cent alcohol per volume. *Una caña* (beer from the tap) is usually cheaper than the bottled variety. *Jerez* or *fino* are both sherries from Andalucia, but you need to be specific about what type is wanted. Spain is a big producer of *coñac* (brandy) – some of the pricier ones are very fine. There is also a wide choice of liqueurs, and Chinchón, within the province, is Spain's leading producer of *aniseed* liqueurs. *Sangría* is a mixture of soda water, red wine, brandy, fruit, fruit juices and ice: pleasant to gulp, it can be very intoxicating.

Non-alcoholic
Many local people drink *agua potable,* drinking water from a tap or fountain. Visitors are advised to drink *agua mineral, con gas o sin gas* (bottled water,

with or without gas). *Té* (tea) is most often served with *limón* (lemon). An *infusión de manzanilla* (hot camomile tea) is both refreshing and supposedly calming. *Horchata,* a cool drink made from ground nuts, is wholesome and refreshing, but an acquired taste. *Granizados* are freshly made and iced fruit juices which slake thirst on a hot summer day. *Zumos* (fruit juices) are available in bottles, cans and cartons; there is a big choice. *Leche* (milk) is usually of the long-life variety, but *leche del día* is also widely available. *Café* (coffee) is a complicated subject in Spain: with milk it is *café con leche.*

Estola, Vega Sicilia, Valbuena and Cava are just some of the wines produced by the Madrid region

FOOD AND DRINK

Where to Eat

The selection of eating places, of all types, which follows is just that – a selection. Many other places justify inclusion. As well as suggesting visits to specific places, the listing takes you to streets and areas where there are other eateries, and gives an idea of the sort of places you can find in Madrid. The emphasis is on restaurants where you can expect to pay less than 6,000 pesetas per person for a three-course meal. Eating places are first shown under city districts, and then described by type of cuisine.

Centro

South of the Plaza Mayor is a host of traditional restaurants and tapas bars. Five recommendations are:

Plaza Mayor, a centre for cafés and bars

Botín, Cuchilleros 17;
Las Cuevas de Luis Candelas, Cuchilleros 1;
Casa Lucio, Cava Baja 35;
Julián de Tolosa, Cava Baja 18; and **La Cacharrería**, Morería 9. To the southeast is **Asador Frontón**, Tirso de Molina 7, and along the Río Manzanares there is **Casa Mingo**, Paseo de la Florida 2. East of Puerta del Sol is another varied clutch:
L'Hardy, Carrera de San Jerónimo 8;
El Cenador del Prado, Calle del Prado 4;
Uhara, Los Madrazo 18;
Armstrongs, Jovellanos 5;
Pereira, Cervantes 16.

North of Gran Vía are three very different places:
Casa Perico, Ballesta 18;
Restaurante Vegetariano, Marqués de Santa Ana 34;
Arce, Augusto Figueroa 22.

Salamanca
El Amparo, Callejón de Puigcerdá 8;
Alfredo's Barbacoa, Lagasca 5;
La Fonda, Lagasca 11;
La Trainera, Lagasca 60;
La Corralada, Villanueva 21;
Brasserie de Lista, Ortega y Gasset 6;
La Estafeta, Núñez de Balboa 75;
Suntory, Paseo de la Castellana 30–38;
Zalacaín, Alvarez Baena 4.
Eastwards from Calle Goya across Calle Doctor Esquerdo are two places worth the trip:
Viridiana, Fundadores 23 and **Or–Dago**, Sáncho Dávila 15. To the south in the *barrio* of Ibiza is **La Tercia**, Doctor Castelo 22.

Chamberi
La Cava Real, Espronceda 34;
Balear, Sagunto 18;
Annapurna, Zurbano 5;
Marinado, Medellín 5;

Modern Madrid
Gaztelubide, Comandante Zorita 37;
Ganges, Bolivia 11;
O'Pazo, Reina Mercedes 20;
Beef Place, Avenida de Brasil 30;
De la Riva, Cochabamba 13;
Chi-Zhi-Ju, Capitán Haya 55;
Alfredo's Barbacoa, Juan Hurtado de Mendoza 11;
Príncipe de Viana, Manuel de Falla 5;
La Fonda, Príncipe de Vergara 211.

> **Choice and Cross Reference**
> Madrid has some 4,000 registered restaurants and 18,000 bars, cafés and cafeterias; many restaurants also have bars, and many bars serve *tapas, raciones* (larger portions) and varied light meals. Many of the cafés, bars and discos listed under **Nightlife** serve snacks or full meals: also consider them. On Sunday nights most restaurants close; others also do so for Saturday lunch, and some shut all day on Monday. During August many (including some of the best), close for a minimum two-week annual holiday; some also close for a few days at Easter, and during Christmas.

Basque
Arce, Augusto Figueroa 22 (tel: 522 5913). Large Iñaki Camba attends to the smallest detail in his serious interpretation of modern Basque cuisine. The prices are honest considering all the attention and the pleasant, modern ambience.

El Amparo, Callejón de Puigcerdá 8 (tel: 431 6456). Charming and professional home of modern cooking, Basque with French inspiration, where it is wise to rely on the suggestions of the maître, Eduardo Navarina. Try for a table on the second floor and expect to pay at least 10,000 pesetas per person for a memorable meal.
Gaztelubide, Comandante Zorita 37 (tel: 533 0214). Although pricey, you will have

FOOD AND DRINK

no complaints after experiencing a meal designed by Jesús Santos in this quietly elegant restaurant, where reservations well in advance are essential. Sr. Santos has perfected a synthesis between the traditional and modern cooking styles of northern Spain which is much acclaimed by Madrid's gourmets.

Julián de Tolosa, Cava Baja 18 (tel: 265 8210). Basque Iñaki Ongay is in charge of the special grill on which the finest quality meats and fish are prepared, and there is a choice of other delicate cooking in this pleasingly modern conversion of an old building.

Or-Dago, Sáncho Dávila 15 (tel: 246 7185). In homely ambience, sample faultless Basque cooking with a quality–price ratio which is hard to beat in Madrid. Booking well in advance is usually essential, and it is well worth the wait.

Zalacaín, Alvarez Baena 4 (tel: 261 5935). It is the Prado of Spain's culinary art, but unlike the museum you have to pay a relatively high price to enjoy the creations here. Masters of modern Basque and international cuisine are Javier Oyarbide and Benjamin Urdiaín,who head the large kitchen team; Liberto Campillo leads the front-of-house performance of catering refinement in intimate rooms of deep-pink hue. The large and well-spaced tables have linen made by a closed order of nuns. With the *menu del día* you can get by for under 10,000 pesetas each, but this is not a restaurant in which to be caring about cost. Its sister, **Príncipe de Viana**, Manuel de Falla 5 (tel: 519 1448), specialises in Basque and Navarra cuisine. It is of a similar high standard.

Restaurant Botín serves excellent food

Castilian

Botín, Cuchilleros 17 (tel: 266 4217). The wood-fired ovens in which the house staples of suckling lamb and piglets are roasted have been alight since 1725 and this may be, as claimed, the world's oldest restaurant. Closely packed tables on several floors are usually crowded with tourists, served by friendly waiters and entertained by a *tuna* – not a fish, but a troupe of young and melodious minstrels in traditional costume. Botín is well-priced for its food, drinks and fun.

Casa Lucio, Cava Baja 35 (tel: 265 3252). A late-19th-century *tasca* (bar), in which big names of politics, entertainment and bullfighting can be seen tucking into simple *huevos con fritas* (eggs and chips) or *callos* (tripe). Getting a table can be difficult.

Las Cuevas de Luis Candelas, Cuchilleros 1 (tel: 266 5428). Close to and much the same as Botín, but not necessarily a second choice to it.

L'Hardy, Carrera de San Jerónimo 8 (tel: 521 3385). One of the city's most renowned eating houses, it was founded as a pastry shop in 1839 and retains a delicatessen section. Upstairs, in elegant rooms (but with service a trifle snobbish), there is a choice of classics like *cocido* (stew), *callos* (tripe) and *chiporones en su tinta* (squids in their ink), and a variety of dishes to meet international tastes. Elevated prices are sustained by the reputation.

Eastern

Annapurna, Zurbano 5 (tel: 410 7727). This high temple of Indian cuisine features an indoor garden as part of its elegance. An extensive choice, finely prepared and with unalarming prices.

Chi-Zhi-Ju, Capitán Haya 55 (tel: 279 9131). Cheap and cheerful Chinese.

Ganges, Bolivia 11 (tel: 259 2585). Modern Madrid's answer to New Delhi or London's best. The décor, service and food, including tandoori dishes, are all impeccable and the cost is very acceptable.

Suntory, Paseo de la Castellana 30–38 (tel: 577 3733). It is pricey but the prepration, presentation and cooking of Japanese food here is of the very highest standard; the ambience is carefully created and the service discreetly attentive. A meal in the Tatami Room will be especially memorable.

Uhara, Los Madrazo 18 (tel: 429 8224). Japanese cuisine and attention at prices which do not empty your pocket.

International

Alfredo's Barbacoa, Lagasca 5 (tel: 576 6271) and Juan Hurtado de Mendoza 11 (tel: 457 8556). Favourite places with the American community and *Madrileños* for their succulent spare ribs and hamburgers, at fair prices.

Armstrongs, Jovellanos 5 (tel: 522 4230). British-inspired international dishes across a

FOOD AND DRINK

wide price range. Sunday brunch is popular with foreigners.

Beef Place, Avenida de Brasil 30 (tel: 556 4187). The name indicates what is available at fair prices in this plain and simply modern eatery.

Brasserie de Lista, Ortega y Gasset 6 (tel: 435 2818). Waiters in long aprons give quick service in the wood-panelled room, from a menu of international and Spanish dishes which has been arranged to appeal to as many as possible. The very fair prices are also appealing.

El Cenador del Prado, Calle del Prado 4 (tel: 429 1549). Expect an above-average price for elegant but relaxed ambience, and dishes of light, modern preparation using the best of what is in season.

Madrid's cafés are ideal places to linger

FOOD AND DRINK

La Cava Real, Espronceda 34 (tel: 442 5432). This is an elegant British-style wine bar, where more than 40 different wines are served as *copas* (by the glass). The thoughtful menus of Ramón Gallego are designed around different wines, at a price of about 7,000 pesetas.

Seafoods

La Trainera, Lagasca 60 (tel: 276 8035). A number of no-fuss rooms is usually packed with locals and tourists enjoying the freshest seafoods, simply prepared and efficiently served at modern prices. Few people are ever disappointed by this 'essential' Madrid meal.

O'Pazo, Reina Mercedes 20 (tel: 253 2333). The ambience is a little dated and prices are quite high, but O'Pazo is irreproachable for the highest quality and freshness of its fish and shellfish, sensitively prepared and pleasingly served.

Spanish – Regional and Mixed

Asador Frontón, Tirso de Molina 7 (tel: 369 1617). A little out of the way, but worth the effort for people wanting perfection in the grilling of finest quality meats at fair prices, in an unpretentious local place.

Balear, Sagunto 18 (tel: 447 9115). As its name implies, the emphasis of this restaurant is on the cooking of the Balearic Islands. Catalan and Valencian rice dishes are also specialities of this homely, well-priced place.

Casa Mingo, Paseo de la Florida 2 (tel: 247 7918). Roast chicken and rough Asturian cider are the only choices in this cheap and busy, basic eatery near 'Goya's church'.

Casa Perico, Ballesta 18 (tel: 531 9199). In an unsavoury area north of Gran Vía, this is an example of a simple Madrid eating place,where the short choice changes daily, the tastes are always savoury, helpings generous and prices at budget level.

De la Riva, Cochabamba 13 (tel: 250 7757). Closed every night, and Saturday and Sunday. Arrive well before 14.00hrs to get a table at Pepe de la Riva's eccentric, cramped eatery where the ever-changing choice is small, good cooking asured and servings generous. Prices, which are generally moderate, are not specified, so remember to check when ordering.

La Cacharrería, Morería 9 (tel: 265 3930). Arrive early to head the line of people in the know about this delightful eatery with its clever salads, homely cooking and fair prices.

La Corralada, Villanueva 21 (tel: 576 4109). Two rooms with rustic and naive décor, where a varied choice of simple Spanish home cooking is served at fair prices, and literary and political people often make lively conversation.

La Estafeta, Núñez de Balboa 75 (tel: 431 8194). Classical and creative cooking under the direction of María Angeles

FOOD AND DRINK

Sánchez from the region of Navarra is attentively served in a pleasant environment. Especially notable is the *menestra*, a mixed vegetable dish in which the flavour of each is separately retained.

La Fonda, Lagasca 11 (tel: 577 7924) and Príncipe de Vergara 211 (tel: 563 4642). Subtleties of Catalan cuisine and a good selection of its wines can be experienced in these carefully decorated and managed places, which maintain moderate prices.

La Tercia, Doctor Castelo 22 (tel: 573 5590). Off the beaten track, this is a homely local eatery where a choice of staple and new Spanish dishes can be sampled at fairly low cost relative to the quality.

Marinado, Medellin 5 (tel: 445 8254). Specialities of this inviting and carefully managed restaurant are Japanese-style foods in their natural state, *crudos* (raw), *carpaccios* and *marinados* (marinated fish). Moderate prices.

Pereira, Cervantes 16 (tel: 429 3934). Luis, Juan and Fina have a simple, friendly and busy eatery giving excellent value. Its choice of Galician dishes includes mainly fish, and local staples like leg of lamb. Arty and political groups often animate the scene.

Viridiana, Fundadores 23 (tel: 246 9040). Fair prices, inventiveness in cooking what is best from the market, and clever presentation, as well as one of the best cellar selections in town, have put Abraham García's slightly off-track restaurant of simple décor among the most deservedly acclaimed and popular. Expect some surprises!

Vegetarian
Restaurante Vegetariano, Marqués de Santa Ana 34, (tel: 532 0927). A full and fresh choice of salads, vegetarian dishes and health drinks at budget prices. Especially good at lunchtime.

Seafood, a speciality

SHOPPING

It is not a good idea to start shopping in Madrid before you have seen the Prado and some of the most notable other sights, for the array of shops and things they sell is so diverse and fascinating that you may become transfixed, and have no time to see anything else during your time in the city. The advice is to concentrate on visiting quaint old speciality and craft shops, boutiques with the *de moda* creations of Spain's acclaimed fashion designers, and commercial galleries, where the talents of contemporary artists can be seen. Also take in a branch of El Corte Inglés and a neighbourhood food market. Do not fail to visit the shopping mall of El Mercado de Puerta de Toledo.

Hours

Most shops are open Monday to Saturday, from 09.30 or 10.00 to 13.30 or 14.00hrs, and then from 16.30 or 17.00 to between 19.30 and 21.00hrs. Some may close on Saturday afternoons, and most do so in the summer. Department stores do not close for lunch. VIPs (drugstore-type mini-markets) stay open until 03.00hrs daily; 7 Eleven branches are open around the clock. A Sunday shopping experience with great contrasts can be had by strolling through **El Rastro**, one of the world's most enlivened street markets, down to one of its most elegant shopping malls, the **Mercado de Puerta de Toledo**. What follows is a brief description of four principal shopping zones, and then a selective listing of where to look for what, which includes street markets.

Shopping Areas

Centro

The central area has a number of different shopping zones. Around the Puerta del Sol and in pedestrianised Calles Preciados and Montera it is very mixed, with department and bargain-basement stores, quality craft, jewellery and clothes shops, a new cultural megastore and some very tacky tourists traps. Along and off Calles Mayor and Arenal, old craft and curiosity shops adjoin down-market outlets serving locals with a whole range of needs, and it is much the same in and around the Plaza Mayor. South of here, down and off Ribera de Curtidores, mainstream of Sunday's El Rastro flea market, are reputable and dubious places selling all sorts of antiques, mock-antiques and plain junk. Nearby is the ultra-chic Mercado de Puerta de Toledo mall. East of Puerta del Sol, Carrera de San Jerónimo and Calle del Prado have some fascinating old-style retailers and pricey art and antique showrooms. Once the city's most fashionable shopping boulevard, Gran Vía still has many varied shops but has lost its grace. Between it and Calle de Génova, especially in Calles Almirante, Conde de Xiquena, Argensola and Orellana, is a concentration of fashion, design and art boutiques showing off the best of Spain's adventurous and acclaimed new talents.

SHOPPING

Salamanca

This is Madrid's Knightsbridge, and Calle de Serrano is its Fifth Avenue. A full spectrum of very high-class shopping can be found along Serrano, and parallel streets: Claudio Coello, Lagasca and broad Velázquez. There is also excellent shopping in the grid of connecting streets. Here, too, are the creations of many of Spain's top talents, as well as most of the leading, and priciest, international brand names.

Argüelles y Bulevares

Northwest of Plaza de España, Calles de la Princesa, Martín de los Heros and other nearby streets have a varied choice of goods including those within an El Corte Inglés department store and the Multicentro Princesa, both near the Argüelles metro station. Also go

An unusual shop front in Plaza Santa Ana

along Calle Alberto Aguilera. Because of its proximity to the university, bookshops abound.

Modern Madrid

Madrid's new Manhattan has its share of good and varied shopping among the skyscrapers: for example, along and linking with Calles Orense and Capitán Haya. Adjoining the Azca commercial development is the Moda shopping mall. Further north, Madrid 2 (La Vaguada) is the city's largest complex, with some 350 outlets of every imaginable type, including a department store, cinemas and places to eat.

Specialist Shopping

Antiques

You need to do a lot of browsing to see the very varied selection and compare prices, which are usually considerably higher in Madrid than in the provinces. See also **Shopping**

Areas (page 85) and **Shopping Malls** (page 90). Two good places to start are **Centro de Anticuarios Lagasca**, Lagasca 36, and **Centro de Arte y Antigüedades**, Serrano 5. Close to many other showrooms are **Abelardo Linares**, Plaza de las Cortes 11, and **Itálica**, Velázquez 54, which specialises in Art Deco.

Art
Spending some time touring Madrid's many *Galerías de Arte* (Commercial Art Showrooms), to see permanent or changing collections, gives a good appreciation of Spain's contemporary art scene: both big names – Tàpies, Antonio López, Miguel Barceló and other *firmas consagradas* (hallowed signatures) – and the up-and-coming. The following leading galleries are in areas where there are many others: **Juana Mordo**, Villanueva 7; **Soledad Lorenzo**, Orfila 5; **Jorge Kreisler**, Prim 13; **Juana de Aizpuru**, Barquillo 44. A number of galleries are now opening in proximity to the 'art triangle' of the Paseo del Prado. For Goya prints from original plates try **Calcografía Nacional**, Alcalá 13.

Books, Newspapers, Magazines and Music
Spain publishes a lot of media products and has a busy recording industry. Apart from many streetside kiosks and book departments in drugstores, packed with reading material, there are interesting bookshops at museums like the Reina Sofía,

and many specialist shops. **La Casa del Libro**, Gran Vía 29, is a traditional bookshop where every Spanish book should be obtainable. **Turner**, Génova 3, specialises in foreign language books. Look for branches of **Crisol,** an innovative and rapidly expanding chain of 'culture supermarkets' whose offerings include music of all types: among its branches are those at Juan Bravo 38, Goya 18 and Paseo de la Castellana 154. **Calle Barquillo** has a string of sound and video specialist shops. A cultural megastore is due to be opened by the French **FNAC** chain on the Puerta del Sol in 1993. Convenient for all official Spanish government and European Community publications is the new **La Librería del BOE**, Trafalgar 27.

Crafts and Local Specialities
For a good general selection look in at **El Caballo Cojo**, Costanilla de San Pedro 7, and **La Tierra,** Almirante 28. Also look in department stores and shopping malls, and be on the lookout for other places in areas where this listing leads you. **Cerería San Sebastían**, Atocha 41, has been making candles since 1760. **Sargadelos,** Zurbano 46, sells the work of acclaimed contemporary ceramicists, and **El Alfa**, Claudio Coello 112, has a selection of classical tiles from Talavera, Manises and Sevilla. **Lladró**, Quintana 2, has a permanent exhibition and sales of Spain's best-known and charming porcelain figurines, etc. **Casa de Diego**, Puerta del

SHOPPING

Sol 12, sells an array of Spanish fans, as well as fine umbrellas and walking sticks. **Hijos de García Tenrio**, Bolsa 9, have been traditional bootmakers since 1886, while **Gil**, San Jerónimo 2, specialise in shawls and handkerchiefs of embroidered silk. **Seseña**, Cruz 23, has been supplying Spanish capes since it opened in 1901. **Casa Yustas**, Plaza Mayor 30, is the place to buy a *sombrero* hat. Local guitar makers include **Felix Manzanero**, Santa Ana 12; **Ramírez**, Concepción Jerónima 2; **Manuel Contreras**, Mayor 80. **La Concordia**, Apodaca 22, opened in 1902 to sell woven grass items and still does so. **Benita Vergés**, Alvarez Mendizábal 29, has pretty dolls and other toys.

Expensive tapestries and rugs can be ordered from the **Real Fábrica de Tapices**, Fuenterrabía 2; others can be bought off the shelf at **Salahonda**, Gaztambide 32. **Artespaña**, a government-sponsored national chain specialising in craft furnishings, has branches at Plaza de Cortes 3, Hermosilla 14, Ramón de la Cruz 33, and at the Madrid 2 (La Vaguada) complex.

Department Stores

El Corte Inglés is Spain's best department store group, with all the usual sections and services of such stores in other countries, including travel agency and shipping services. Inner-city branches are at Preciados 3; Princesa 41; Goya/Alcalá; Raimundo Fernández Villaverde 79.

Nibbles and Drinks
See these quaint old shops and buy things to eat yourself, or give as gifts. (The year of opening is in brackets.)
Casa Mira, Carrera de San Jerónimo 30, has Jijona *turrón* (nougat) (1841). Other traditional sweets are sold at **La Pajarita**, Villanueva 13 and Puerta del Sol 6 (1881).
Horno del Pozo, del Pozo 9, makes delectable *hojaldres* (puff pastries) and *empanadas* (pies) (1830).
Pecastaing, Príncipe 11, has wines, spirits, liqueurs and delicatessen items (1886).

Design, Gifts and Mementoes

Again, be on the lookout all the time, because there are a lot of fascinating things available – both useful and decorative. You are likely to find something appealing at:
B D Ediciones de Diseño, Villanueva 5;
Idea Madrid, Paseo de la Habana 24; and
Atico, Cea Bermúdez 70.

Drugstores

Jumbo 24, Avenida Pío XII 2, is open 24 hours, throughout the year, and has a restaurant, cafeteria, book and recordings shop, plus a photo-processing shop and a food and drinks shop. Spread throughout the city, and offering broadly similar services, are branches of **VIPs** and **7 Eleven**.

Fashions

Spain has moved into the forefront of the fashion world

and it is one of the many pleasures of Madrid to see the creations of its leading designers; more so to buy some. Look especially along and off Calle Almirante, in the Salamanca district and in the shopping malls. The following designer shops are not to be missed.

For Men and Women
Adolfo Domínguez, Serrano 96, Ayala 24, Ortega y Gasset 4, Mercado de Puerta de Toledo;
Antonio Alvarado, Caballero de Gracia 22;
Francis Montesinos, Argensola 8.
For Women
Agatha Ruiz de la Prada, Marqués de Riscal 8;
Coal, Valenzuela 9;
Irene Pada, Columela 3;
Purificación García, Velázquez 55;
Sybilla, Jorge Juan 12;
Teresa Ramallal, Almirante 5;
Elena Benarroch, Monte Esquina 18.
For Men
Jesús del Pozo, Almirante 28;
Pedro Morago, Almirante 20.
For Children
Chiquitines, Padre Damián 18;
Friki, Velázquez 35.
Jewellery
Joaquín Berao, Conde de Xiquena 13;
Yanes, Goya 27;
López, Calle del Prado 3.

Food and Drink
As *Madrileños* care much about this subject, there are many very tempting shops and local fresh-food markets which are a delight to visit for colour and bustle. A few suggestions across the city:

Fruit markets abound

El Riojana, Mayor 10 (pastries and desserts).
Palacio de Quesos, Mayor 53 (cheeses – Spain has some 350 different types).
Museo de Jamón, Carrera de San Jerónimo 6 (*jamón serrano* – mountain ham, from all over Spain).
Madrueño, Postigo de San Martín 3 (wines from Madrid province, as a special memento).
Rincón del Cava, María de Guzmán 43 (an exceptional selection of sparkling *cavas*).
Herbolario de la Fuente, Pelayo 70 (herbs mixed to order).

SHOPPING

Mallorca, Velázquez 59 y
Serrano 6 (luxury supermarket,
with good choice of prepared
foods and fine pastries).
Santa, Serrano 56 (sweets).
Vázquez, Ayala 11 (wondrous
displays of quality fruit and
vegetables).
Ilintxa, Fernando el Santo 4
(a delicatessen: Basque and
French eats and drinks).
Semon, Capitán Haya 23
(smoked salmon and Catalan
delicatessen products).

*High-quality goods are sold in
Madrid's malls*

Malls
These are recent developments
of striking design, with small
outlets selling high-quality
merchandise; mainly fashion,
design, art and antiques. Their
eating places are also stylish
and there are spaces for
(usually) interesting exhibitions.
Mercado de Puerta de Toledo,
Ronda de Toledo, a very chic,
converted fish market with 140
shops, is now an 'essential'
sight of the city (open Sundays
but closed Mondays); **Galeria
del Prado**, Carrera de San
Jerónimo (Palace Hotel), has

around 40 up-market boutiques; and smaller, but sparkling new, is **El Jardín de Serrano**, Goya 6 y Claudio Coello 37. **Moda Shopping**, Azca Center, is accessible from Paseo de la Castellana and Calle Orense, and has 100 shops within its glassed-in mall. More down-market are **Multicentros,** Serrano 88, Orense 6 and Princesa 47 (the latter is especially good for cheap and cheerful fashions for the young).

Markets
Arts and Crafts
Plaza de Santa Ana. Daily.
Books
Cuesta Claudio Moyano, adjoining the Jardín Botánico off Paseo del Prado. Daily, but best on Sunday for second-hand Spanish and foreign books.
Fleamarket
El Rastro, Plaza de Cascorro, Ribera de Curtidores and surrounding streets. Friday, Saturday, and best on Sunday. Hundreds of stalls selling everything imaginable amid the cacophony of raucous vendors and bargain-hunters. These days pickings are few (unless you are a pickpocket), and much is junk, but a visit is immense fun, and bargaining part of it.
Food
Mercado de Sant Miguel, off Calle de Mayor. Weekdays. Worth visiting to see a fascinating display of fresh foods in an attractive iron and glass building.
Stamps and Ephemera
Plaza Mayor. Sunday mornings for stamps, coins and old postcards.

ACCOMMODATION

Madrid's hotels of good international standard are now among the most expensive in the world, but many of them have lower rates at weekends and deal with holiday operators, which allows ordinary people to enjoy their hospitality. Quite a few pretentious but mediocre hotels hang on to the skirts of the top ones. At the bottom end of the market there are many clean and comfortable rooms in *hostales, pensiones, fondas* (inns) and *casas de huéspuedes* (guest houses): some of the best only accept guests on personal recommendation, and therefore cannot be included in listings which follow. A large number of budget places to stay are in seedy parts of town and are best avoided. (See **Crime** in the **Directory**, and also refer to **Tight Budget**.) No matter what category of accommodation you want, it is always helpful to get suggestions from people who have had a satisfactory stay in Madrid. Travel agents can give advice, but make sure it is not biased for commercial reasons; lists of hotels can be consulted at Spanish tourist offices in your country, but they will not make bookings. The same applies to tourist offices in Madrid. Hotel reservation agencies operate at Barajas airport and at Chamartín railway station. Confirm all prices before making a commitment. It is acceptable to ask to see bedrooms before committing yourself. As a rule, you will do better by booking on a 'room

ACCOMMODATION

An imposing entrance

only' basis. Breakfast in a nearby bar will be cheaper than in a hotel, and is an opportunity to be among local people. And as eating out is one of Madrid's 'essential' experiences, you do not want to be committed to taking all your meals in the same place. A selective listing of establishments across a wide price range in different city districts follows.

5-star

Ritz, Plaza de la Lealtad (tel: 521 2857), Gran Lujo, 160 rooms, Trust House Forte. Men must wear ties beyond reception and *belle époque* splendour reigns in the public rooms; spacious bedrooms and bathrooms are delightfully dated; and there is great attention to detail in amenities, decoration and service by a staff proud to be part of this Madrid institution which King Alfonso XIII had built in 1910. The restaurant, one of Madrid's best, offers a French-inspired international cuisine, and the summertime *terraza* is a fashionable feature for drinks and light or full meals. So is brunch on Saturday and Sunday. Residents have access to golf and other amenities at the exclusive Club Puerta de Hierro.

Palace, Plaza de las Cortes 7 (tel: 429 7551), 518 rooms, Ciga. Across the *paseo* from the Ritz, and at about half its cost, the historic Palace has all the amenities and good service of a grand hotel, with a distinct personality that makes it a favourite of people from the worlds of politics, arts and entertainment. Many a rendezvous is made in the handsome rotunda room.

Wellington, Velázquez 8 (tel: 575 4400), 295 rooms. Near the Puerta de Alcalá and convenient for the Salamanca district and Parque del Retiro, this independent, traditional and recently modernised hotel is well-priced for what it offers in comfort and service. It has a quiet garden and a swimming pool. Ask for rooms on upper floors, overlooking quieter Calle Villanueva.

Santo Mauro, Zurbano 36, (tel: 319 6900), Gran Lujo, 37 rooms, Cadena NH. Madrid's latest offer for ultimate indulgence has prices on a par with the Ritz. It is a recent conversion of a ducal palace built in 1894. Original features coexist with modern decoration, comforts and gadgetry. Spacious bedrooms have very big beds. An indoor pool and gymnasium are part of the offer. Service is superb. Dishes from País Vasco and Navarra predominate in the Belagua restaurant, part of which was once the palace's beautiful panelled library. (For central reservations for other 4-and 3-star hotels in Madrid in this chain, tel: (93) 417 3232.)

Meliá Castilla, Capitán Haya 43 (tel: 571 2211), 1,000 rooms, Sol Hotels. Among modern Madrid's skyscrapers is the uninspiring, huge block of this hotel. Inside it is plainly functional and efficient. It has relatively fair prices in its 'full-service offer', which is the hallmark of this chain catering largely for business and package-holiday guests. (For central reservations for other 5- 4- or 3-star hotels in this group, tel: 571 5040.)

4-star
Gran Hotel Reina Victoria, Plaza del Angel 7 (tel: 531 4500), 200 rooms, Tryp Hotels. A fine early 20th-century building with large casement windows overlooking the *plaza*, recently extensively and elegantly remodelled to make it the best bet in this animated part of the city. It has traditionally been a stomping ground of people in the bullfighting business; hence its

Bar Taurino, where those sort of people gather. (For central reservations for other 4- 3- or 2--star hotels in this group, tel: 315 3246.)

Suecia, Marqués de Casa Riera 4 (tel: 531 6900), 128 rooms, Best Western. Unremarkable but efficient, comfortable, well-priced and very convenient for the 'art triangle', theatreland and other nightlife.

Gran Velázquez, Velázquez 62 (tel: 575 2800), 130 Tryp Hotels. A conservative and creaky *grande dame* of Salamanca, like some of the local ladies who take tea in its *salón*. Comfortable and reasonably priced, and very well situated for shopping and restaurants.

Los Galgos, Claudio Coello 139 (tel: 562 6600), 358 rooms, Sol Hotels. Modern, comfortable and efficient at the top end of one of the city's most delightful and interesting shopping and residential streets.

Breton, Breton de los Herreros 29 (tel: 442 8300), 57 rooms, Cadena NH. Fresh and bright hotel at fair prices but with limited amenities, in the smart area of Chamberi. Ask for one of the back rooms overlooking the gardens.

Holiday Inn Madrid, Plaza Carlos Trías Beltrán 4 (tel: 555 5162), 313 rooms. Adjacent to the Azca centre of modern Madrid, and little different from Holiday Inns elsewhere, it has a good quality–price ratio.

3- 2- and 1-star
Reyes Católicos, Calatrava 32

ACCOMMODATION

(tel: 265 8600), 3-star, 38 rooms. This is a good choice if you want to be near the sights, bars and restaurants of old Madrid, the Mercado de Puerta de Toledo and El Rastro. It has recently been pleasantly renovated and, although there is nothing fancy on offer, it has everything you will probably want during your stay, at a fair price.

Inglés, Echegaray 8 (tel: 429 6551), 3-star, 58 rooms. Basic, clean, comfortable and not over-priced, at the heart of a clutch of good eating and drinking places.

Santander, Echegaray 1 (tel: 429 9551), 1-star, 39 rooms. More simple and an even cheaper choice in this fun area of Madrid

Elegant Gran Hotel Reina Victoria

Mora, Paseo del Prado 32 (tel: 239 7407), 2-star, 39 rooms. If you want to be close to the 'art triangle' and live on a classy *paseo*, this is a good choice.

Coruña, Paseo del Prado 12 (tel: 429 2543), 1-star, 10 rooms. It may be difficult to get one of the basic rooms in this small hostel on the prime *paseo*.

Mediodía, Plaza Emperador Carlos V 8 (tel: 527 3060), 1-star, 161 rooms. This big and bustling hostel, convenient to Atocha station and the 'art triangle', is all right for a short stay.

Mónaco, Barbieri (tel: 522 4630), 1-star, 32 rooms. The price is above average for the extravagant touches and romantic air in this eccentric, somewhat jaded hostel in a

shopping and nightlife district.

Ramón de la Cruz, Don Ramón de la Cruz 94 (tel: 401 7200), 2-star, 103 rooms. On a quiet street near Calle Alcalá in Salamanca's southeast corner, this agreeably priced, modern and basic hotel has few foreigners as guests. A good choice of restaurants is close by, and so is the Parque del Retiro.

Marcenado, Marcenado 9 (tel: 519 0338), 1-star, 23 rooms. Northeast of Salamanca near Ciudad Jardín is this example of a neighbourhood hostel, giving simple comfort at a low price and surrounded by inexpensive local bars, shops, eateries and restaurants.

Airport Hotels

There are three in proximity to Barajas airport which belong to the same chain. (For central reservations, tel: 747 7700.) **Barajas**, Avenida de Logroño 305 (tel: 747 7700), 5–star; **Alameda**, Avenida de Logroño 100 (tel: 747 4800), and **Diana**, Galeón 27 (tel: 747 1355), both 3-star.

Apartment Hotels

These offer self-catering facilities, as well as most usual hotel services, and are economical for visitors planning longer stays. **Foxá 25** and **Foxá 32**, Augustín de Foxá 25, 32 (tel: 733 7064, 733 1060). Convenient to Chamartín railway station and modern Madrid. **Recoletos**, Villanueva 2 (tel: 431 9540). Enjoys a privileged position just off Paseo de Recoletos.

NIGHTLIFE

The desiccated nightscene of Franco's capital was sparked like a tinderbox by the flame of freedom from dictatorship. Madrid is again the trend-setting capital of the Spanish-speaking world, an avant-garde European city where an appreciation of culture in all forms, and a feverish pursuit of other pleasures or undemanding leisure, can be wholly indulged through long nights. Statistics support Madrid's claim that its people get by with less sleep than other Europeans, and visitors become heavy-lidded in staying on the prowl as long as *los gatos*, the cats of Madrid's nightscene, who are still bright-eyed at dawn.

The first fact to face is that, as in the rest of Spain, Madrid's nightlife starts late – around the time when many other European cities are shutting down. *Los Beautiful* (trendsetters) frequent their favourite haunts during the week, largely abandoning them to the plebeians at weekends. Different parts of the city have very different atmospheres; different social groups follow different routines, which change with the seasons. It is essential to be fashionably dressed, dressing down rather than up, and not to be short of cash, real or plastic – for the best of Madrid's nightlife has a high price tag. It is preferable to be with a partner, more so with a group, and wise to move between different parts of the city by taxi.

NIGHTLIFE

An Essential Trawl

Besides partaking of the wide cultural offerings always available in Madrid, there are some essential things to do to get a taste of the city's nightscene. A night trawl can begin with a *copa* (drink) at the **Círculo de Bellas Artes** or a *coctel* (cocktail) in the **Museo Chicote**. Continue by going from one *tasca* (bar) to another in the area south of the **Plaza Major** to sample different *tapas.* Follow them with dinner in the same area, to enjoy Castilian staples in an old *mesón* (inn) like **Bótin**. Move on to the usually lively scene around **Plaza de Santa Ana** and down **Calle de las Huertas**, popping in where the scene and sounds attract. In the warm months take a long stroll along the 'Costa de Madrid', the **Paseos del Prado**, **Recoletos** and **Castellana**, with their dozens of *terrazas,* each with its own ambience and regular groupies. They are lively under the stars until the early hours. As a last stop on a nocturnal odyssey take in one of Madrid's classic discos like **Pacha**, **Archy** or **Joy Eslava**. When dawn is breaking, revive yourself a little with *churros con chocolate* at an early-opening *chocolatería*. If it is high summer, head out one night on the Carretera de La Coruña to the sizzling social scenes at the **Hipóteca de la Zarzuela** horseracing track. Alternatively, visit **Oh Madrid** disco with its poolside parade of beautiful bodies, or, further out, the **Casino de Madrid**, which also has a disco and is a popular haunt of *los Beautiful.*

Close to Heaven

It is not long before a visitor to Madrid comes across the boast *de Madrid al cielo*, which roughly means Madrid is the next place to heaven. It is a reasonably fair presumption by the *Madrileños*, considering that, at 2,150 feet (655m) above sea level, theirs is the highest capital city in Europe. Although a thickening film of air pollution is increasingly separating the city from the thin and dry air above, on many days the sky still retains a memorable luminescence. By night, the stars sparkle like diamonds, almost there for grabs, but the sky is at its most strikingly beautiful when day is changing to night. Spectacular sunsets can make you feel so good to be alive that you want to celebrate all night. A good place to start the celebration is in the **Parque del Oeste**, with its vistas to the pink-lit Sierra de Guadarrama. This could be followed by a leisurely drink at one of the *terrazas* along **Paseo del Pintor Rosales**, which from May to October is known as the 'Costa del Oeste'. Or you can simply take in the view from the Sky Garden terrace of the Hotel Plaza.

The listings that follow are of places where different types of live performances are presented. Bars, discos and other venues, where the customers are the entertainment, are grouped together in areas. The listing is, of necessity, very

Bars are essential to Madrid's nightlife

selective. It concentrates on places which are just that bit more 'special', have shown staying power, or look as if they have it. In addition to seeing what is on at the venues below, you should check with billboards and the media to find out what is on at other places in the city, which include open air venues in the warm months. (See also **Special Events** and **Directory**.) **Galicia Ticket Agency**, Plaza del Carmen 1 (tel: 531 9131) sells tickets for some theatres, special events, football and basketball games, as well as bullfights. Tickets for big concerts can often be bought at special box offices in branches of El Corte Inglés department stores.

Opera, Concerts, Dance, Theatre

Principal venues are under the auspices of national, regional and municipal governments, or of cultural foundations (mainly those of banks). The Orquesta Sinfónica y Coro Nacional de España, as well as international orchestras and choral groups, perform in the new and large **Auditorio Nacional de Música,** Príncipe de Vergara 146, where the acoustics are the best imaginable. On Calle Atocha, the **Teatro Monumental** is the usual venue for the Orquesta Sinfónica y Coro de Radio Televisión Española. A new home for the Ballet Nacional de España is within the large and interesting **Complejo Cultural Arganzuela,** the freshly converted abattoir of Matadero de Legazpi along

Paseo de la Chopera, where Madrid's own symphony orchestra and chorus are also based. After the costly and controversial refurbishment of the Teatro Real, Madrid now has a highly specialised venue for opera in the **Teatro de la Opera** on the Plaza de Oriente. An essentially Spanish cultural experience is going to be the *zarzuela*, a spicy form of operetta about the lives of ordinary people, which began in Madrid during the 17th century. In summer, try to see a performance in traditional **La Corrala**, at the heart of the *castizo* district. The **Teatro Lírico Nacional de la Zarzuela,** Jovellanos 4, is the country's main venue for this frothy entertainment of light opera and chirpy dialogue; it also has its own ballet company, orchestra and choir. The **Nuevo Apolo** (Teatro Musical de Madrid), Plaza Tirso de Molina, is a commercially sponsored venue for *zarzuela* and other music and dance forms. Adaptable for all types of stage presentation, and including a full orchestra pit, is the high-tech **Teatro de Madrid**, Avenida Ilustración, in the northern district of La Vanguada. It is the newest cultural venue of the *Ayuntamiento* (municipality) which also has the multi-space **Centro Cultural de La Villa,** Plaza de Colón, for a variety of cultural presentations. Dramatic works of a high standard, on the site of a 16th-century playhouse, are performed at the municipally sponsored **Teatro Español**, Plaza de Santa Ana. It also has an experimental space, theatre, video and book library, and the appealing Café del Príncipe. Belonging to the *Comunidad de Madrid* are the **Teatro Albeniz**, de la Paz 11, where music and dance, both classical and contemporary, are presented; and the **Infanta Isabel,** Barquillo 24, where youth theatre is promoted. Companies and theatres under the auspices of Spain's Ministry of Culture are: the **Centro Dramático Nacional** (Teatro María Guerrero), Tamayo y Baus 4, for contemporary Spanish and foreign drama, as well as live music in its Café Teatro; **Compañia Nacional de Teatro Clásico** (Teatro de la Comedia), Príncipe 14, which presents classical Spanish works; and **Centro Nacional de Nuevas Tendencias** (Sala de Olimpia), Plaza de Lavapies, where the latest theatrical trends have an opportunity to flourish. Other alternative theatre venues include **Ensayo 100 Teatro,** Gravina 11, **Sala Pradillo**, Pradillo 12, and **Sala Artea**, San Gregorio 8. Brand new, and with a capacity for 25,000 to see all types of *grandes espectáculos,* is the **Auditorio del Parque de la Hinojosa**, Campo de las Naciones (near Barajas airport).

Cinema

Carmen Maura, Antonio Banderas and Pedro Almodóvar, the director, are just three bright international stars of the Spanish film industry, which yearns for more government support to compete with the American domination of Spain's screens.

The **Ciudad de la Imagen**, in Pozuelo de Alarcón, is an area of some 3 million square feet (279,000 sq m), where Madrid's audio-visual industry is encamping. Local film fans frequent the **Filmoteca Española (Cine Dore)**, Santa Isabel 3, its bar-restaurant and bookshop.

Most foreign films are dubbed: original soundtracked versions, VOs, can be seen at the multi-screen **Alphaville** and **Renoir** complexes on Calle Martin de los Heros, near the Plaza de España, and at a few other cinemas.

Shows, Dinner and Dancing

Look in media listings under *salas de fiesta* and *espectáculos*. Some places to consider are: **Scala Melia Castilla**, Rosario Pino 7 (tel: 571 4411), which has big international cabaret shows, with or without dinner, followed by dancing. **Florida Park**, Avenida de Menéndez Pelayo, Parque del Retiro (tel: 573 7804), is less pricey for its shows of Spanish ballet and flamenco. **Casa Patas**, Cañizares 10 (tel: 369 1574) has a bar, restaurant and *tablao* late on Thursday, Friday and Saturday nights, which is much appreciated by real *aficionados* of flamenco. Other venues for flamenco, with dinner as an option, are **Café de Chinitas**, Torija 7 (tel: 248 5135), a touch exclusive and expensive, and **Corral de la Morería**, Morería 17 (tel: 265 8446), to which most tour groups are taken. *Sevillanas*, the flamenco-derived dances now so fashionable throughout Spain, are flowingly performed

Cinema in Gran Vía

by practised exponents in *salas rocieras*. Watch them on three dance floors, and try out your own body movements at **Sierra Morena**, Paseo Reina Cristina 7 (tel: 501 6107). For gentle dancing to the sounds of yesteryear a middle-aged crowd gathers at **Golden Boite**, Duque de Sesto (tel: 573 8775). Out of town is the very elegantly refurbished, multi-space **Casino de Madrid**, Carretera de La Coruña (tel: 856 1100), with dining (including barbecues some nights), a choice of gambling (passport required) and disco dancing. A coach service is provided for guests, from Plaza de España.

NIGHTLIFE

Live Music (*Música en vivo*)
Classical
An essential spot for a touch of sophisticated Madrid nightlife is the **Palacio Gaviria**, Arenal 9 (tel: 526 6069), a lovingly restored 1850s palace, where you can enjoy concerts while sipping an expensive drink, or view art shows in the chapel. Others are **La Fídula**, Huertas 57, and the nearby **Salón del Prado**, del Prado 4.

Spanish and Latin American
Café Libertad, Libertad 8, is a pleasant place to hear a variety of Spanish popular music. **Café del Mercado**, Mercado Puerta de Toledo, is an 'in' spot for *ritmos calientes y latinos*.

Jazz
Main mecca is the Art Deco **Café Central**, Plaza del Angel, where two-hour sets start nightly at 22.30hrs. Not far away are two more popular places: **Café Jazz Populart**, Huertas 22, and **Johnny Jazz Club**, Cervantes 7. In the Salamanca district just off Paseo de la Castellana is **Whisky Jazz Club**, Diego de León 7, another venue for good jazz.

Rock and Pop
Large concerts with big-name performers from Spain and abroad are held at **Universal Sur**, Parquesur, Leganés, seven miles (11km) south of the city; **Auditorio de la Casa de Campo**, which has a capacity for 60,000; **Palacio de Deportes,** Jorge Juan 99; **Ciudad Deportiva Real Madrid**, Paseo de la Castellana 259; and **Plaza de Toros de Las Ventas**. Intimate venues usually worth checking out include **Universal Club**, Fundadores 7,

Wealth is on display at Joy Eslava disco

and **Agapo**, Madera 22, for a variety of pop and rock; **Revolver Club**, Galileo 26, for nostalgic rock 'n' roll; and **Canciller,** Alcalde López Casero 15, for fans of the heaviest stuff.

Cafés, Tabernas, Bars, Discos

There are many more places where *los gatos* frolic, but you can start with these suggestions within three areas. Also refer to the **Food and Drink** section, and to venues above, to plan your night out.

East of Puerta del Sol, between Calles Alcalá and Atocha

This area bubbles with nightlife, especially near Plaza de Santa Ana and along **Calles Huertas** and **Moratín**. More places are opening in proximity to the 'art triangle' of the Paseo del Prado. Some stops not to be missed: **Círculo de Bellas Artes,** Marqués de Casa Riera 2, whose café and terrace are busiest with an arty crowd between 17.00 and 23.00hrs. Two other animated cafés are **Café Galdos**, Los Madrazo 10, and **Café de las Letras**, Santa María 37. Three traditional *tabernas* (taverns) include **Viva Madrid**, Manuel Fernández y González 7, which has a beautiful façade with early 20th-century tiling; **Los Gabrieles**, Echegaray 17, with Andalucian tile decoration of the 1920s; and red-faced **Casa Alberto**, Huertas 18, which dates from 1827. At **Chenel**, Atocha 107, *maestro* Antoñete has given his name to a place where he is celebrated. **Candela**, corner of Calles Olmo

and Olivar, south of Atocha, has a mainly gypsy clientèle which keeps it lively and noisy into the early hours. In complete contrast, **Stella**, Arlabán 7, is a redoubt of bright sparks, where the style of music changes nightly and there is a bowling alley below the disco.

West and South of Puerta del Sol

Another concentration of varied nightscenes. The Tex-Mex **Mecalito**, Plaza de la Morería, specialises in Mexican drinks. Wealth and success are on display at **Joy Eslava**, Arenal 11, a long survivor on the disco scene. **Taberna de Antonio Sánchez**, Mesón de Paredes 13, is almost 200 years old and has a beautiful, welcoming interior. Other old-time places are **Casa Antonio**, Latoneros 10, where flamenco and bullfighting *aficionados* have been gathering since 1890; and **Casa Vacas**, Cava Alta 23, an old stabling inn which retains its large gates. Two attractive cafés close together are **La Bobia**, San Millan 3, and **Café Bailen**, Bailen 19. Nearby are the summertime *terrazas* of Las Vistillas.

Between the streets of Gran Vía, Fuencarral, Génova and Paseo de Recoletos

A big mix of places, including quite a few close to Plaza Chueca which almost exclusively attract gay people. **Museo Chicote**, Gran Vía 12, is the city's most legendary bar, retaining all the Art Deco features from its opening in 1931. **Casa Sierra**, Gravina 11, is a 1930s tavern and **La Taberna del Alabardero,** Fernando V 6, is a modern model of an old-style one. Two very high-fashion scenes are **Big Bamboo**, Barquillo 42, and **Hanoi**, Hortaleza 81, which has an especially strict door control. **Pacha**, Barceló 11, has long been a favourite disco of *los Beautiful*. Not to be missed along the Paseo de Recoletos are the stylish **Café Espejo** and the unpretentious and legendary **Café Gijón**, and, on warm nights, their busy *terrazas*. Moving north into **Paseo de la Castellana** are more summertime *terrazas*. Off Castellana, **Calle Juan Bravo** has a host of haunts attracting some of the youngest pacesetters. A converted theatre, **Teatriz**, Hermosilla 15, with its highly modish, multi-level interior by Philippe Starck, is a paradise for poseurs and gawpers, while **Archy**, Marqués de Riscal 11, has a different ambience and is the ultimate yuppie temple. **Karaoke Hakodate**, Fortuny 47, where less timid guests take the microphone, has been very much 'in' since it was favoured by a visit from handsome bachelor Príncipe Felipe, heir to Spain's crown.

Sex and Shows

Madrid is not short on naughty or plainly pornographic entertainment for all tastes, and local listings in the media provide information for those who want it. There are sex-for-sale propositions of all types at varying prices, but visitors are advised to avoid them. The health risks may be greater than any short-lived pleasure.

WEATHER AND WHEN TO GO

The climate is continental, which means there is a big contrast between the heat of high summer and the cold winters. The average maximum daily temperature in summer is 30°C (86°F), in contrast with 10°C (50°F) in winter, but the peaks of summer and troughs of winter can be considerably higher and lower. The Sierra de Guadarrama is a barrier to cold northerly winds in winter, so snow is not a regular part of the city's scene then. In summer, gentle winds blowing from the same mountains have some effect in lowering the temperature and clearing the air. Autumn is the season of highest rainfall, which comes mostly in short thunderstorms. Spring is certainly the most pleasant season climatically, when the skies are usually clear, humidity is low and temperatures are comfortable.

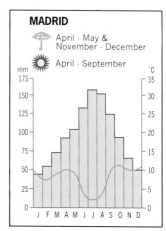

MADRID

☂ April · May & November · December

☀ April · September

HOW TO BE A LOCAL

Madrid is Spain's big mixing bowl of people from all parts of the country. Two inpourings of migrants doubled the population in the 20 years to 1970, and have diluted the numbers of 'genuine' *Madrileños.* Spain's post-war poverty drove many rural people to seek better lives in towns and cities during the late 1940s and early 1950s; as Spain's economic boom developed in the next decades, another wave of migrants arrived, in search of work in new businesses within the province. Many of the newcomers had not intended to stay, hoping only to improve their lot and then return to their places of origin. Certainly, living conditions in the shanty slums which arose around the

Hard at work in Plaza Mayor

southern flanks of the city, in dilapidated inner-city areas, were no inducement to stay. But the great majority did stay, tied to commitments and routines, in the hope of material progress and the promise of much better opportunities for their children. Most of the slums have now been replaced by housing estates with blocks of subsidised apartments. Some migrants have moved rapidly upwards on the ladder of economic and social progress, into smarter housing and integration through marriage with non-migrant families. Perhaps because it gives them a stronger sense of identity among an urban mass, people from beyond Madrid, and even

HOW TO BE A LOCAL

A 'genuine' Madrileño

They are also known for their sharp wit. Like London's cockneys, they have a distinct form of speech, and the traditional dress of the men is very similar to that of a costermonger. Contrasting with them, and other-working class communities spread through the city, are the families with 'old wealth' and/or titles, who head the traditional social scene. Other families have bred successive generations of bureaucrats, professionals and intellectuals to administer, guide and educate the nation. More so in the past than now, men enjoyed *tertulias,* regular gatherings for animated discussions in their favourite watering holes, like the Café Gijón. Coiffured ladies still chatter together over afternoon tea while indulging in fattening sweets in *salóns de té.*

With the coming of democracy, its cultural and intellectual reawakening and the modernisation of its businesses, Madrid has had an influx of very bright sparks from around the country, and some from abroad. With Madrid-born people of the same ilk – politicians, bankers, business leaders, 'yuppies', academics, artists, designers, nightspot owners, and entertainment stars – they are Madrid's new trendsetters, the so-called *los Beautiful.* They work and play hard in Madrid during the weekdays and long nights; weekends are to recover, or to rush off to some distant pleasure spot.

Short-time visitors cannot hope to get an understanding of the

their children born in the city, would rather say they are from so-and-so than admit that Madrid is their home town. They support bars, restaurants, clubs, cultural associations, festivities, banks and service industries which are associated with their region of origin, like Andalucia or Galicia. At holiday times they abandon Madrid and head 'home'. Some migrants and their children have made no progress in the city, and have become trapped in crime and drug addiction.

Ever-ready to define themselves as *Madrileño,* and even to claim that they are the only true ones, are the *castizos* who live in a close community within and around Lavapiés.

subtleties of Madrid society and will find it difficult to gain access to a social group. Spaniards are generally hesitant about giving newcomers access to their family or associates. Matters can be helped by avoiding certain topics of conversation until you are sure of your ground: the Civil War, current politics, bullfighting and football. These issues cause sharp divisions of loyalty. People can be highly critical of all aspects of Madrid and of Spain, and they may slander their institutions, politicians and functionaries – but find it offensive if outsiders are too critical. It is very difficult for most Spanish men to admit that their opinions or actions may be wrong or inappropriate, and apologies are very rare. Like people in other big cities, *Madrileños* are preoccupied with making things go right for themselves in a crowded, fast and competitive environment, and irritability thresholds can be low at times, especially in the heat of summer. Tourists with time on their hands may find a sharp remark or curt behaviour offensive when it is not intended to be so.

Something else to get used to, and not complain about, is the city's time schedule, especially the *siesta* (which breaks up the day), and the late eating times at night. It really is very enjoyable slipping into the same routine. Visitors to Madrid should expect to find preoccupations and general behaviour similar to those in other big European capitals. And the best advice is to be, as always, yourself. Do not try too hard to be a 'local'.

CHILDREN

Like other Spaniards, *Madrileños* are very welcoming and tolerant towards children. Public and private bodies arrange a wide range of educational events for children, but it is usually not easy for visiting children to gain access to all that is on offer. Tourist offices can provide information on current programmes and refer you to relevant organisations. They can also advise about *guarderías*, daytime care centres, and parents will probably enjoy Madrid's principal attractions more without having bored and tired children in tow. The following are among places and activities which children will enjoy. Check locally for current opening days and hours.

Acuario, Maestro Victoria 8. The aquarium has a wide selection of fish and aquatic animals, including crocodiles. *Metro*: Callao.

Casa de Campo. *Madrileño* families go to this extensive parkland for walks, games and picnics in delightful surroundings. There are also other amenities and attractions which make this the top spot for children: **Madrid Zoo** has over 3,000 animals, including pandas, performing dolphins and a Children's Zoo, where animals can be fed and petted. *Open:* 10.00hrs to sunset.

Parque de Atracciones has all the fun of the fairgrounds including a roller-coaster and a big wheel. Entertainment events are held in the auditorium.

CHILDREN

Open: 12.00–19.00hrs (an hour later on Saturday). **El Lago** is a lake where there are rowing boats and canoes for rental, and nearby there is a swimming pool. Children will most enjoy going to the Casa del Campo on the **Teléferico** (cablecar), which operates from the Paseo del Pintor Rosales between 12.00–18.00hrs. Other ways of reaching the Casa del Campo are *Metro:* Lago or Bátáno, *Bus:* 33 and 65.

Lagosur, Carretera de Toledo, Leganés. Diversions in this open-air and covered amusement park 5½ miles (9km) from the centre include carts, a roller-coaster and circus acts, as well as an aquatic park.

Children are welcomed in Madrid

Open: 17.00–24.00hrs weekdays; from 12.00hrs weekends.

Minigolf, Montesa 11. *Open:* 15.00–20.00hrs. *Metro:* Manuel Becerra.

Museo de Cara, Paseo de Recoletos 41. Wax figures of Spanish and internationally famous personalities and animated scenes. *Metro:* Colón.

Museo Nacional de Ciencias Naturales, José Abascal 2. Permanent and temporary exhibitions of natural sciences, specially designed to be of interest to young people. *Metro:* Quevedo.

Museo Nacional de Ferrocarril, Paseo de las Delicias 61. Gleaming steam engines are among the exhibits here, which portray the development of rail transport. *Metro:* Atocha.

Parque del Retiro. The opportunities for family fun in this inner-city green space include hiring rowing boats on the *estanque* (lake), rides in a *calesa* (horse-drawn carriage), watching puppet shows, street performers and pavement artists, and enjoying the playgrounds. *Metro:* Banco.

Planetarium, Parque Tierno Galván. Showings in this modern planetarium are educational and entertaining for all ages. *Metro:* Méndez Alvaro.

Safari Madrid, Reserva El Rincón, Aldea del Fresno, CN V via Navalcarnero. Animals roam in this small reserve, others perform in shows.

TIGHT BUDGET

Find out what budget holiday packages to Madrid are available from your country: these often work out far cheaper than arranging travel and accommodation yourself. If you are entitled to a student card, get one and find out what discounts can be derived with it, both in travelling to Madrid and once you are in the city. Travel agents specialising in youth travel can advise about low-cost independent travel by air, coach or rail, and about cheap accommodation. If you are looking for accommodation on the spot, there is a big choice available at tourist offices, where you can also get advice on free entertainment, discount schemes for students and the like. It is always wise to check out a room before committing yourself to accommodation. A good area in which to start looking is in the *barrio* of Cortés, east of Plaza de Santa Ana, and between Calles Alcalá and Atocha. This area is very convenient for principal sights, including the 'art triangle', has budget eating places and a young, spirited nightlife. Argüelles, Universidad and Gaztambide, on either side of Calle de la Princesa, are other parts favoured by students and budget travellers. Within this area is the Youth Hostel at Calle Santa Cruz de Marcenado 28, close to Argüelles metro station. Other parts of the city also have budget accommodation and eating places, but bear in mind their accessibility and the cost of travelling to places of interest. Also note that areas present different aspects by day and night: Malasaña, for instance, is a quiet neighbourhood during the day, but at night it can be somewhat threatening.

● Avoid places which display an array of credit card signs.
● Ordering a choice of *tapas* or *raciones* (larger portions) can be more costly than the *menu del día*.
● Beer is cheaper if you ask for *una caña* and a *vino de la casa* will be the lowest priced.
● Buy food and drink in a market or shop to make up a picnic which you can enjoy in one of the city's open spaces, like the Parque del Retiro.
● Keep a small supply of food and drink in your room as a standby.
● Walking is the cheapest and best way of getting to know the city, but also use the bus and metro networks. Buy saver tickets (see also the **Directory**).
● For excursions beyond Madrid, use buses or trains, or make up a party with like-minded people and rent a car or minibus.
● Join *Madrileños* in enjoying free entertainment, while being a part of it, for instance, by doing people-watching.
● Make the most of the cost by lingering over your drink at fashionable bars, *terrazas* and discos, as the locals do.
● For budget shopping, avoid high-class districts and tourist areas.

SPECIAL EVENTS

In this ever-active city, on every day of the year, there will be notable special events catering for different interests. Different districts also have their own popular festivities, mainly of interest to their inhabitants. More and more events are continually being added to the city's annual calendar. The following listing describes some of the major events of the year.

January
The New Year opens with a lively celebration in the Puerta del Sol. On the 5th the **Three Kings** distribute sweets to children in procession .

February
ARCO – the Contemporary Art Fair – is a leading event for top artists, dealers and collectors worldwide. The popular celebration and partying of **Carnival** ends on Ash Wednesday.

March
The **International Theatre Festival** presents styles from around the world. In this month, or in April, there are also solemn **Holy Week processions.** A **Jazz Festival** is run by a college of the university. The bullfighting season begins at **Las Ventas** until October.

April
A three-month-long **Mozart Festival** starts, and there is an **Antique Music Week. Cumbre Flamenca** is a celebration of the best of flamenco, while **FINART**, an International Crafts Fair, also takes place. The

International Festival of Imaginary and Science Fiction Films shows the latest examples of this genre.

May
On the 2nd, Madrid remembers its uprising against Napoleon in 1808. **Book fairs** offer the newest, second-hand and antique publications. From the 8th to the *Día de San Isidro* on the 15th there are **traditional festivities** in celebration of the city's patron saint. **Rock and Jazz festivals** are organised by the *Villa de Madrid.*

June
From the 9th to the 13th, **San Antonio de la Florida** is honoured with popular festivities. **Los Veranos de la Villa**, running through to September, is a season of music, theatre, *zarzuela*, dance and open-air cinema which takes place under the auspices of the *Villa de Madrid.* **Madrid Dances** features top international, modern and classical dance companies.

July
Several districts have celebrations in honour of La Virgen del Carmen.

August
In the week up to the 15th, the feast day of La Virgen de la Paloma, the *castizo* neighbourhood of old Madrid is lively with locals celebrating and dancing the energetic *chotis* in traditional dress.

September
The **Autumn Festival of Music, Theatre and Dance**, sponsored by the *Comunidad de Madrid,*

begins for three months.There is also a festival of *Madrileño* theatre in the last fortnight of this month. In the first week, **Pasalera Cibeles** takes place. It is a parade of fashion and design by Spain's leading names. **Youth Week** features film, theatre and musical performances.

October
Seasons of orchestral and chamber music, running through to March, open at the **Auditorio Nacional** and **Teatro Monumental.** At the **Teatro Lirico Nacional de la Zarzuela**, the season of opera, *zarzuela* and ballet begins and continues to July.

November
The **International Jazz Festival** attracts performers and fans from around the world. On the 9th the city marks the **feast day** of its patroness, Nuestra Señora de la Almudena.

December
From the middle of the month the Plaza Mayor is packed with stalls selling Christmas decorations and small gifts. **Christmas Eve** is celebrated with a family dinner at home and, perhaps, Midnight Mass. On the 25th, restaurants are packed out for lunch. On the 28th, **Día de los Inocentes**, friends play tricks on each other and the media indulge in elaborate hoaxes.

Football is still the most popular sport in Madrid, and Real Madrid has a huge following; Atlético de Madrid is its equally popular rival

SPORT

It seems a long time ago that *fútbol* (football) was just about the only sport which had a significant following in Spain, and when it also had political connotations due to General Franco's manipulative support of the Real Madrid club. Spaniards now feature as champion performers in many sports, and the country's somewhat delayed arrival on the international sports scene has meant that the many sports facilities that have mushroomed in recent years are of modern design and the highest standard.

Spectator sports
Major **championship events** in football, golf, tennis, cycling, squash and other sports can be seen in Madrid, mostly between March and June.

Athletics (*Atlético*)
Big events are usually held at the **Estadio Vallehermoso**, Calle Juan Vigón 10.

SPORT

Basketball (*Baloncesto*)

Spain's second-biggest national spectator sport can be seen at **Palacio de Deportes**, Calles Jorge Juan 99; **Ciudad Deportiva Real Madrid**, Paseo de la Castellana 259; and **Polideportivo Magariños**, Calle Serrano 127 (also a venue for handball matches).

Football (*Fútbol*)

Strong rivalry exists between Madrid's two premier clubs, whose successes or failures can affect the mood of the city: **Real Madrid** is at home in the Estadio Santiago Bernabeú on the Paseo de la Castellana; **Atlético de Madrid** is based at the Estadio Vicente Calderón on the Paseo de los Melancólicos alongside the Río Manzanares. Cavalcades of hooting cars and street celebrations follow the successes of these clubs.

Horseracing

Daytime racing is held from February to June and mid-September to early December. In the summer, the **Hipódromo La Zarzuela** is one of the top spots of Madrid's nightlife, and there are races from around midnight to 02.00hrs. The Hipódromo is 5 miles (7.5km) from the city, on Carretera de la Coruña. On race days a bus service operates from the Plaza de España.

Motor Racing

Circuito de Jarama, Carretera de Burgos, 17 miles (27km) from the city is the venue for car and motorcycle races.

Pelota

Exciting matches of the fast Basque sport of *jai-alai,* on which spectators bet, can be seen at the following *frontón* courts: Calle Dr Cortezo 10; Avenida Moratalaz 40; Calle Villanueva 2.

Participant Sports

Almost every sport can be enjoyed at public or commercial amenities in or near the city. Some installations of the *Villa* or *Comunidad de Madrid* can be used by visiting sportspeople. Information and advice about all sports and amenities can be obtained from the **Instituto Municipal de Deportes,** Palacete de la Casa de Campo, Fuente del Rey (tel: 464 9050). Amenities of the nearby **Club de Campo Villa de Madrid**, Carretera de Castilla (tel: 207 0395), include a golf course, tennis courts and stables, with horses for hire.

Wintersports.

The closest resort is Navacerrada, in the Sierra de Guadarrama, some 30 miles (50km) from the city. Information about it and three other wintersports resorts, can be obtained from offices in the city: **Navacerrada,** Casado del Alisal (tel: 230 5572); **Valcotos,** Felipe IV 12 (tel: 239 7503); **Valdesquí,** San Ramón Nonato 1 (tel: 215 5939); **La Pinilla** (in the province of Segovia), Paseo de la Castellana 173 (tel: 270 6731).

Watersports.

Information about amenities for waterskiing and sailing on lakes and reservoirs within the *Comunidad de Madrid* can be obtained from: **Federación Castellana de Esquí Náutico,** San Andrés 36 (tel: 448 0695).

Directory

This section (with the biscuit-coloured band) contains day-to-day information, including travel, health and documentation.

Contents

Arriving
Camping
Crime
Customs Regulations
Disabled Travellers
Driving
Electricity
Embassies and
  Consulates
Emergency
  Telephone Numbers

Entertainment
  Information
Health
Holidays
Lost Property
Media
Money Matters
Opening Times
Pharmacies
Places of
  Worship

Police
Post Office
Public Transport
Senior Citizens
Student and Youth
  Travel
Telephones
Time
Tipping
Toilets
Tourist Offices

Arriving
Entry Formalities

You require a valid passport to enter Spain. Nationals of European Community countries do not need a visa, and neither do nationals of many other countries for stays of up to 90 days. Rules are ever changing so it is wise to check the current situation with a Spanish tourist office or Spanish Consulate in your country. Visitors from most countries do not require any medical documents but, if in doubt, check with one of the above. To obtain visas or permissions for extended stays in Spain, contact the **Oficina de Visados para Extranjeros,** Los Madrazo 9 (tel: 521 9350).

By Air

Madrid's *Aeropuerto de Barajas* is the hub of the international and domestic network of Iberia, Spain's national airline. National and independent airlines operate scheduled connections with Madrid. Seats are also available on charter flights, bringing customers of package-holiday operators. There can be great variations in the cost of flights; it is always helpful to spend some time checking out options. Connections with Spanish cities are by Iberia or Aviaco, its affiliate, and competing independent companies have also appeared. Iberia runs a *Puente Aereo,* air-shuttle

DIRECTORY

service, between Madrid and Barcelona and Madrid and Sevilla (Seville). Barajas airport is 10 miles (16km) east of the Puerta del Sol, off the N 11 highway to Barcelona, and has separate terminals for international and domestic flights. Although a little dated, it has the usual amenities of a Grade 1 international airport, including a tourist office, hotel reservation desk and car-hire facilities. Porters charge by the number of bags. Between 04.45 and 01.15hrs, a scheduled bus connects every 15 minutes with a terminal below the Plaza de Colón. A high-technology train link with the station of Nuevos Ministerios may be operating in 1993. Licensed taxis are usually plentiful and relatively inexpensive. (For airport Information, tel: 205 4372.)

By Bus

Enquire at budget travel agencies and Spanish tourist offices in your country about coach services to Madrid from other European countries. It is likely that there will be an increasing number of services in future, following great improvements to Spain's highway network; and due to increased traffic from Britain after completion of the Channel Tunnel.

By Car

It is along highways N I (Madrid–Irán) and N II (Madrid–Barcelona) that most foreign drivers arrive in Madrid, from the north and northeast respectively. To Valencia in the east is the N III; to Cádiz and Sevilla in the south there is the N IV; and to the Badajoz (and Portugal) in the west there is the N V. To go to La Coruña, in the northwest, there is also the N VI. A motorway ring around Madrid connects these routes with one another. The local signposting

Puerta de Alcalá

tends to assume that all drivers have a good sense of direction and a knowledge of local geography. Get your bearings before getting close to Madrid. Avoid arriving in the city on Sunday afternoons and evenings during the summer months, or after any long weekends, when long lines of traffic stack up on the approach roads.

By Rail
Renfe is Spain's national rail company, and its services are being greatly improved. Connections across the French border are on either side of the Pyrenees: at Irán in the Basque country (west) and at La Jonquera in Catalunya (east). An AVE high-speed train connection from Madrid to Catalunya is planned, to link up with the French high-speed system and with an AVE track already operating to Sevilla. Talgo trains are the fastest and most comfortable on normal services. Other trains can be a slow way of seeing the country. Trains from the north arrive at Madrid's Charmartín station, while those from the south use the remodelled Atocha station. The two stations are connected by a direct rail service, which stops at Recoletos and Nuevos Ministerios. Travel is cheaper on certain days (*Día Azul*) and at certain times of the day or night, so remember that it is worth checking locally for these details.

Camping
There are four well-serviced sites within 6 miles (10km) of the city centre, open all year.

One is the **Arco Iris**, Carretera Villaviciosa–Boadilla (tel: 616 0387). More details are available from Spanish tourist offices in your country, and from the **Federación Española de Empresarios de Campings,** Gran Vía 88, 28013 Madrid (tel: 242 3168), which will make reservations.

Chemist see Pharmacies

Crime
Madrid does not have the feel of a threatening city, except in a few specific areas, but there are incidents of street crime in all parts, even the smartest. The need to finance drug dependence is usually the motivation. Snatching handbags and cameras, picking pockets, running off with unattended luggage or parcels and breaking into cars are the principal crimes visitors should be aware of. Mugging for jewellery or cash also happens. Most people should not attempt to resist mugging, as the criminal is usually armed and desperate, and may be operating with others. The precautions to take are obvious: deposit valuables (traveller's cheques, cash, passports, etc) in a safe where you are staying; wear your handbag and or camera across your chest, and put your wallet in a front trouser pocket; do not be ostentatious with jewellery or cash; keep an eye on your shopping, even when sitting at a smart café, and on your luggage; keep car doors locked at all times, even when driving; do not leave valuables in a car (a bag holding nothing of value may

DIRECTORY

be temptation for a break-in, if left in sight); avoid lonely, seedy and dark areas; and use taxis late at night. Finally, be aware and look aware.

Areas in which to take special care (more so at night), where it is best not to walk alone, are those at the western end of Gran Vía and in streets off it, especially to the north in the *barrio* of Malasaña. Also be careful in and around Puerta del Sol, Plaza de España, Plaza Mayor and Plaza de Oriente. Metro stations and trains are best avoided at night. Petty criminals flock where crowds gather, like the El Rastro market.

Customs Regulations

These are in line with those of other European Community countries. Personal effects can usually be taken into Spain without payment of duty. There is little point in taking in the small amounts of wine, spirits and tobacco permitted, as they are generally much cheaper to buy in Spain. For information on current allowances and regulations, consult your airline or holiday operator, a Spanish tourist office or the Spanish Consulate in your country. In Madrid the **Customs Office** is at Calle Guzmán el Bueno 137 (tel: 254 3200).

Disabled Travellers

Newer buildings are likely to have amenities such as ramps, wider doorways and toilets for the disabled. These are now also provided in many places of interest, including the museums of the 'art triangle'. Special needs should be stated and full enquiries made before making final reservations for travel and accommodation. Organisations for disabled persons in your country will have useful advice, and Spanish tourist offices will be helpful.

Driving
Breakdown

Special arrangements may be provided by an insurance policy bought from your motoring organisation. Many of these organisations have reciprocal arrangements with **Real Automóvil Club de España** (RACE), José Abascal 10, 28003 Madrid (tel: 445 6205). There is also a '**Help on the Road**' service (tel: 742 1213). In the case of hired vehicles, contact the hire company. Towing trucks are called *gruas* and a repair shop is a *taller.* Yellow page telephone directories have listings of these, as well as main agents for different makes of cars. A 24-hour tyre and lighting repair service is given by **Tallers Arancha**, Dolores Barranco 86 (tel: 269 8231).

Car Hire

Holiday operators have car-hire schemes and airlines offer 'fly-drive' deals. Big international firms operate in Madrid, and you can make bookings with them in your home country. Main inner-city offices, plus the Barajas airport telephone numbers of three of them, are as follows: **Avis**, Paseo de la Castellana 57 (tel: 447 0579; airport 205 4273); **Europcar**, General Yagüe 6 (tel: 556 1500; airport 205 5163); **Hertz**, Jacometrezo 15 (tel: 542 1000; airport 205 8452). **Italcar**,

Alcántara 59 (tel: 401 3019) and **Atlas**, General Varela 35 (tel: 270 0854), are good, low-price hirers; **Alcalá**, Alcalá 118 (tel: 401 6546) provide chauffeur-driven Cadillac and Mercedes limousines; **Regente**, Paseo de la Reina Victoria 13 (tel: 534 1004) hire cars, vans and mini buses; while **Motoalquiler**, Conde Duque 13 (tel: 542 0657) have mopeds, scooters and motorcycles.

It is always advisable to have full damage-waiver insurance.

Documents

Licences issued by European Community countries are acceptable. People from other countries should have an international driving licence, usually obtainable from motoring organisations in their country. Drivers should always have with them their driving licence, car registration and insurance documents and rental agreement, if applicable.

Driving in Madrid

Avoid it whenever possible, to save yourself much frustration and so as not to add to the city's traffic congestion and air pollution. It also takes some time to get used to the dangerous eccentricities of local drivers. Because the *siesta* interrupts the day, the city has four rush hours. In 1980 the daily average speed in the city was 34 miles per hour (54kph); now it is down to 13 miles per hour (21kph).

Fuel

The fuel sold is normal (92 octane); super (96 octane); gas-oil (diesel); and *sin plomo* (lead-free).

Check parking restrictions before going shopping

Parking

Street parking is indicated by blue road and kerb markings, and tickets are bought from nearby machines. Most of the 1.2 million *multas* (fines) issued by the *Ayuntamiento* are for illegal parking, but only eight per cent of fines are actually ever paid.

Attempts are being made to rectify this situation, so do not be tempted to join the locals in breaking traffic laws. Car parks are spread around the city and it is wisest to use them.

Road Signs and Rules

Legislation which became effective in June 1992 has put road signs and rules even more

DIRECTORY

closely in line with those of other European countries, but there are still differences which are only comprehensible after exposure to them. Spain's Ministry of Transport publishes a small leaflet giving advice to drivers. Try to get one at frontier posts or tourist offices.

Electricity

220/230 volts AC generally, and 110/120 in some older buildings. Plugs have two round pins.

Embassies and Consulates

Most nations are represented in the city. Get listings from the **Diplomatic Information Office** (tel: 266 8605), tourist offices or the police.

Canada, Núñez de Balboa 35

Repair work is sometimes carried out during public holidays

(tel: 431 4300).
Republic of Ireland, Claudio Coello 73 (tel: 576 3500).
UK, Fernando el Santo 16 (tel: 319 0200).
US, Serrano 75 (tel: 577 4000).

Emergency Telephone Numbers

Policia Nacional
091
Policia Local
092
Bomberos (Fire)
080
Medical Emergency
061
Ambulance
479 9361

Clearly state your name, the nature of the *urgencia* (emergency), your location and the services required. See also **Health** and **Police**.

Entertainment Information

In addition to taking note of billboards and picking up leaflets and information from tourist offices, you can consult the daily newspapers and their weekly supplements (see **Media**). The weekly *Guia del Ocio* and monthly *La Capital* also have comprehensive listings. Or contact the **Foreign Language Information Service** (tel: 435 1844).

Entry Formalities
see **Arriving**

Health

Residents of European Community countries are entitled to medical care from the Spanish health service, if they have form E110, E111 or E112 from their national health service (obtain this before departure). Madrid has five

large public hospitals with *urgencia* (emergency) departments: quite central, east of Parque del Retiro, is the **Hospital General Gregorio,** Ibiza s/n (tel: 576 8000). Eight public **first-aid centres,** open 24 hours a day, are spread across the city: in the centre there is one at Calle Navas de Tolosa 10 (tel: 521 0025). All foreign visitors to Spain should buy a travel insurance policy from a reputable company, to provide comprehensive cover in case of accident or illness. **ASTES**, Núñez de Balboa 101 (tel: 262 2087) provides reliable policies.
It is also wise to carry a photocopy of prescriptions for any medication which you are taking. There are a number of private hospitals and clinics to which you may be directed locally, or by your insurers: one is the **Unidad Médica Anglo-Americana**, Conde de Aranda 1 (tel: 435 1823), where 24-hour general medical attention by bilingual staff is available.

Holidays
Principal public holidays are:
Año Nuevo: 1 January
Día de los Reyes: 6 January
Jueves Santo: Easter – variable
Viernes Santo: as above
Día del Trabajo: 1 May
Dos de Mayo: 2 May
San Isidro Labrador: 15 May
San Juan: 24 June
Santiago: 25 July
Asunción: 15 August
Hispanidad: 12 October
Todos los Santos: 1 November
Señora de la Almudena: 9 November
Día de la Constitución: 6 December
Inmaculada Concepción: 8 December
Navidad: 25 December

Lost Property
Contact the **Oficina de Objetos Perdidos**, Plaza de Lagazpi 7 (tel: 588 4346). Advise your consulate about any loss of personal documents and, if necessary, contact credit-card companies. Also report losses at a police station and obtain a copy of the report, if you intend to make an insurance claim.

Media
Periodicos (Newspapers) and Revistas (Magazines)
Many newspapers from other European countries are available in Madrid by the afternoon. International editions are on sale in the morning. The 'liberal' *El País* is Spain's biggest national daily, widely respected internationally. Among other national dailies are the 'middleground' *El Mundo, Diario 16* and the 'conservative' *ABC*. 'What's On' booklets are issued by *El País* on Thursdays and by *El Mundo* and *Diario 16* on Fridays. Spain publishes a plethora of magazines. The weeklies *Tiempo* and *Cambio 16* are among a number of good news and feature magazines. *Hola* is the leader of a pack of personality and gossip weeklies. Most leading magazines from Europe and the US are also widely available.

Television and Radio
Two channels, *TVE-1* and *TVE-2* are national and state-run; one, *Tele Madrid,* is sponsored

by the *Comunidad de Madrid*; and *Tele-5*, *Antena-3TV* and *Canal Plus* (subscription) are private stations. Check the programmes of *TVE-2* for times of news programmes in English, French and German. The programmes of many European satellite broadcasters and CNN can also be received. Foreign, national, regional, local – public and private – radio stations vie for space among the airwaves. From 06.00–08.00hrs, Monday to Saturday, Radio 80 (89FM) has an English news and entertainment programme.

Money Matters
Banks
Bancos and *Cajas* (savings banks) are everywhere in Madrid, and many foreign banks also have branches in the city. *Open:* Monday to Friday 08.30–14.00hrs, Saturday (except June to September) 09.00–13.00hrs. A few big branches stay open until 16.30hrs, Monday to Friday. Currency-exchange facilities are available outside these hours at the airport and main railway stations. Cashpoints, issuing money around the clock with the use of a cash or credit card and PIN, are to be found everywhere.

Credit Cards
The major credit, charge and direct debit cards are widely accepted, Visa most widely. In case of queries or losses contact **American Express** (tel: 279 6200); **Diners Club** (tel: 247 4000); **Eurocard/Mastercard** (tel: 435 3040); or **Visa** (tel: 435 3040).

Currency
The *peseta* is available in the following denominations: notes – 10,000, 5,000, 2,000, 1,000; coins – 500, 200, 100, 50, 25, 10, 5 and 1.

Tax
IVA, a value-added tax, is currently applied at 6 per cent on most goods and services and at 15 or 28 per cent on luxury items and some services. People resident outside Spain can gain exemption from tax on large, individual purchases. Shops can provide more information. But remember to think about what tax the goods may incur on importation into your home country, too.

Opening Times
See also the **Shopping** and **Food and Drink** sections, and **Money Matters** and **Post Office** in this **Directory**. Businesses work Monday to Friday 09.00–14.00 and 16.00–20.00hrs. In the summer many businesses work *horas intensivas*, 08.00–15.00hrs. Official organisations are generally open to the public Monday to Friday, 09.00–13.00hrs.

Pharmacies
As well as selling prescription medicines, *farmacias* provide free advice about minor injuries or ailments and can suggest non-prescription treatments from their stocks. They are easily identified by a big green or red cross sign, and follow normal shopping hours. At other times they display a sign indicating the nearest *farmacia de guardia* which is open. Local

papers also list them; or tel: 098.

Madrid is rich in art galleries

Places of Worship
For information about religious services, tel: 541 4804. Or visit your embassy.

Nearly all churches are Catholic, with services in Spanish. Catholic Masses in English are said daily at 10.30hrs at Calle Alfonso XIII 165. There are also services at the **British Embassy Church of St George** (Anglican), Núñez de Balboa 43 (tel: 276 5109), and religious ceremonies at the **Jewish Community**, Balmes 3, (tel: 445 9835). The **International Protestant Community**, can be found at Padre Damián 34 (tel: 445 0684).

Police
Officers of the three police organisations have different, but sometimes confusingly overlapping roles. See also **Emergency Telephone Numbers**, page 116.

Policia Local
The municipal police are mainly responsible for traffic. They have blue uniforms and white checked bands on their vehicles and caps. (Tel: 588 5000.)

Policia National
Spain's national police, also in blue, are responsible for law and order in larger urban areas, and for internal security. It is to one of their *comisarias* that you should report a crime or loss, and make a *denuncia* (statement), which is necessary for insurance purposes.

Guardia Civil
Officers in olive-green uniforms are mostly seen at border posts, guarding some public buildings in country areas; and along the coastline. A branch of the organisation is responsible for highway patrols.

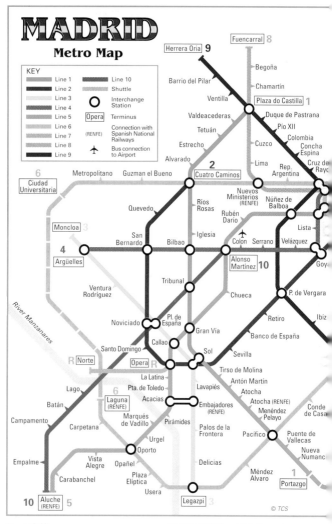

Post Office

The main *Correos* (post office) (Palacio de Comunicaciones) is on Plaza de la Cibeles (*Open*: Monday to Friday 09.00–14.00 and 16.00–19.00hrs, Saturday 09.00–13.00hrs.) Mail can be sent addressed to you at: Lista de Correos, Palacio de Comunicaciones, Plaza de la Cibeles, Madrid, Spain. Take personal identification with you

Map user No. 9C/02/117

when collecting mail. Post boxes are yellow and some have different sections for different destinations. *Sellos* (stamps) can also be bought at *estancos* (tobacconists).

Public Transport

Air

Travel agents are the best source of information, at no extra cost. Quite a few foreign airlines have offices in Madrid. The main office of IBERIA is at Calle Velázquez 130 (tel: 587 8787), and there are branch offices elsewhere. (For information, tel: 411 2545.)

Bus and Coach

EMT, the municipal transport company, operates some 1,800 buses between 06.00–24.00hrs, and a few all-night *buhos* (owls). Single fares are bought on the bus. Information booths operate at Puerta del Sol, Plaza del Callao and Plaza de la Cibeles. *Bonobus* saver tickets (for 10 trips) can also be bought from them, and from *estancos* (tobacconists).

Various companies operate scheduled coach services to nearby towns, and to all parts of Spain. Details are available from tourist offices. The main coach terminal, Estación Sur de Autobuses, is on Calle Delicias. *Metro:* Palos de Frontera.

Metro

EMT has six interconnecting metro lines, with 120 stations operating from 06.00–01.30hrs. Some of the comfortable trains are air-conditioned. Tickets can be bought at station ticket booths or machines.

Taxis

Madrid's 15,000 licensed taxis are black or white, with a red stripe, and have the *villa's* coat-of-arms on their doors. They show a green light and a *libre*

DIRECTORY

The Palacio Cristal can be reached on foot from Parque del Retiro

(free) sign when they are available for hire. Standard rates are shown on the meter, and there are supplements for baggage, for trips at night and for those departing from railway stations or the airport. **RadioTaxi** (tel: 547 8200); **TeleTaxi** (tel: 445 9080).

Trains

Madrid has three mainline station complexes with comprehensive amenities, which include left-luggage lockers. **Charmartín,** Augustin de Fox (tel: 323 1515) connects Madrid with the north and east; **Atocha**, Plaza de Carlos V (tel: 527 3160) connects it with the west and south, including the AVE high-speed train terminal;

and **Norte** (formerly **Príncipe Pío**), Paseo del Rey (tel: 247 0000), connects it with the northwest. Train or metro lines link these stations, from which *cercanias* (local trains) also operate between 05.30–23.00hrs. Full information can also be obtained from travel agents, and from **Renfe,** Alcalá 44 (tel: 429 0202 – Spanish only). Renfe operates a number of trains for day and weekend excursions (see also **Excursions from Madrid** on page 54**)**.

Senior Citizens

Check with travel agents what special package holidays for senior citizens are available, either in Madrid itself, or in tours of Spain including Madrid. It is difficult to gain access to Spanish organisations for senior citizens, or to their projects and entertainment programmes.

Student and Youth Travel

Consult with specialist travel agencies, tour operators and youth organisations in your own country. See also **Tight Budget.** In Madrid, tourist offices can refer you to local youth organisations and advise you of current projects and programmes. (For general information and reservations for youth hostels, *Albergues Juveniles*, tel: 521 4427.) There are many private language schools which arrange accommodation for their students. For information about the offer of an official school, contact **Departamento de Español para Extranjeros**, Escuela Oficial de Idiomas, Jesús Maestro s/n, 28003 Madrid (tel: 254 4492).

Telephones

Many hotels provide telephone and other services, but add large supplements. The code for seven-digit numbers in Madrid (city and province) is **91**. This is used for calls from other provinces. To call a Madrid number from outside Spain dial the international service code applicable in your country, then 34 (Spain), 1 (Madrid) and the seven digit number. Public phone booths are plentiful and are being updated; many take phone cards, which can be bought at *estancos* (tobacconists). Instructions for use are displayed in a number of languages, as are provincial and international dialling codes. Many bars also have telephones for use by customers. To make direct international calls, put at least 200 pesetas in the groove at the top (or in the slot of some telephones), or insert the phone card, dial 07 and wait for a changed tone. Then dial the country code, town code (without an initial 0) and the number. (For general information, tel: 098.) You can get assistance, make reverse charge calls and pay after your call at Telefónica Locutorios, Gran Vía 30; Paseo de Recoletos 41; Virgen de los Peligros 19; and at the main *Correos* (Post Office).

Telefax, Telex and Telegrams

Business bureaux offer telefax and (some) telex services. The central telegram office is at the main post office, where fax and telex services are also available. (For telegrams by telephone – 24-hour service – tel: 522 2000.)

Time

Like most of Europe, Spain is . two hours ahead of GMT (Greenwich Mean Time) in the summer, and one hour ahead in the winter.

Tipping

Although most hotel and restaurant bills will include a service charge, you may still want to give a tip of between five and ten per cent in restaurants, and for special services in hotels. At bars leave around five per cent or less from whatever change you get. The same applies to taxis. Other people who usually get tips are car-park attendants,

DIRECTORY

doormen, hairdressers, lavatory attendants, shoeshiners and tour guides.

Toilets
Public lavatories are few and far between. There are toilet facilities at department stores and at some museums and places of interest. Bars and restaurants also have facilities for the use of their customers. Standards are variable.

Tourist Offices
Turespaña of Spain's Ministry of Tourism operates offices in:
Australia: 203 Castlereagh Street, Suite 21, Sydney NSW 2000.
Canada: 102 Bloor Street West, 14th Floor, Toronto.
UK: 57–8 St James Street, London SW1A 1LD.
US: 665 Fifth Avenue, New York 10022; 8383 Wilshire Bvd, Suite 960, Beverley Hills, California 90211.

In Madrid
Municipal, Plaza Mayor 3 (tel: 266 5477).
Comunidad, Torre de Madrid, Plaza de España (tel: 541 2325), and Duque de Medinaceli 2 (tel: 429 4951).
Aeropuerto de Barajas, Llegadas Internacionales (International Arrivals), (tel: 205 8656).
Estación de Charmartín (tel: 215 9976).

Sightseeing is a tiring business

LANGUAGE

In order to improve their job prospects or simply to be more modish, many young *Madrileños* have been rushing to language schools to learn foreign languages (by far mostly *inglés*), and some have been abroad to study. But it remains rare to hear anything but Spanish spoken by the older generation, and by shop assistants and waiters of any age.

Castilian is a language in which a word is generally pronounced as it looks, and exceptions are few. Correct grammar is obviously very desirable, but correct pronunciation and word stress are the key factors.

Pronunciation
Vowels
a – as in **tar**
e – as in **let**
i – as in **marine**
o – as in **Tom**
u – as in **rule**

Consonants
These are pronounced like those in English, but there are some important exceptions: **b** and **v** – similar, and pronounced like a soft 'b'; **c** – pronounced like the 'k' in keep before an *a*, *o*, *u* or consonant in Spanish, but like the 'th' in thin before a Spanish *e* or *i*; **g** – like 'g' in get, but before an *i* or *e* in Spanish it is like *j* below; **h** – always silent; **j** – like the 'ch' in loch, but silent at the end of a word; **ll** – like 'll' in million; **ñ** – like 'n' in onion; **q** – like 'k' in keep (always followed by silent *u*); **r** – strong and rolled, **rr** more so; **y** – like 'y' in yes; **z** – like 'th' in thin.

Word Stress
Words ending in *n*, *s* or a vowel have the stress on the second-to-last syllable. Other words carry stress on the last syllable. An acute accent on the syllable to be stressed denotes exceptions to the above rule. Accents are also used to differentiate between words of similar spelling, but different meaning.

Useful Words and Phrases
It is obviously not much use asking a complicated question if you will not understand the reply. This short list will be helpful to show courtesy, understand signs, ask directions, do shopping and order services. The person may speak your language, so ask.

hello hola
I am sorry but I don't speak Spanish (or only a little) lo siento, pero no hablo español (o solamente un poco)
do you speak Danish, Dutch, English, French, German, Italian? habla danés, holandés, inglés, francés, alemán, italiano?
is there someone who speaks... hay alguien que habla...
yes/no sí/no
excuse me, I don't understand perdón, no comprendo
please speak slowly por favor, hable despacio
thank you (very much) (muchas) gracias
you're welcome/think nothing of it de nada
good morning buenos días
good afternoon buenas tardes
good evening buenas noches
I am/my name is soy...../me llamo...

LANGUAGE

Music has a language of its own

what is your name? como se llama usted?
how are you? como está?
good/bad bien/mal
I am... estoy...
very well muy bien
I (don't) know (no) sé
I (don't) know (a person) (no) conozco
alright vale/de acuerdo
good luck buena suerte
goodbye adiós
see you again hasta luego
where is...? donde está?
is it far/near? está lejos/cerca?
very muy
left/right/ahead/at the end izquierda/derecha/delante/al final
avenue/boulevard/road/street/passage/square avenida/paseo/carretera/calle/pasaje/plaza
countryside/mountain(s)/hill/river/stream campo/montaña (sierra)/colina/río/arroyo

castle/church/monastery/palace/school castillo/iglesia/monasterio/palacio/escuela
open/closed abierto/cerrado
hour/day/week/month/year hora/día/semana/mes/año
Monday to Sunday lunes, martes, miercoles, jueves, viernes, sabado, domingo
yesterday/today/tomorrow ayer/ hoy/mañana
last night/tonight anoche/esta noche
the weekend el fin de semana
last week/Next week semana pasada/ semana próxima
early/late temprano/tarde
I would like... me gustaría...
I'm looking for... busco...
I want... quiero...
I need necesito
do you have...? tiene...?
there is (not) (no) hay
how much (cost)? cuánto es/vale/cuesta?
expensive/cheap caro/barato
short/long corto/largo
enough/too much bastante/demasiado
more/less más/menos
good/better bueno/mejor
big/bigger grande/más grande
small/smaller pequeño/más pequeño
nothing more, thank you nada más, gracias
zero to 20 zero, uno, dos, tres, cuatro, cinco, seis, siete, ocho, nueve, diez, once, doce, trece, catorce, quince, dieciseis, diecisiete, dieciocho, diecinueve, veinte, **21** veintiuno, **30** treinta, **32** treinta y dos, **40** cuarenta, **50** cincuenta, **60** sesenta, **70** setenta, **80** ochenta, **90** noventa, **100** cien, **200** doscientos, **500** quinientos, **1,000** mil.

INDEX

INDEX/ACKNOWLEDGEMENTS

ACKNOWLEDGEMENTS

The Automobile Association wishes to thank the following photographers and libraries for their assistance in the preparation of this book.

MARY EVANS PICTURE LIBRARY 8 Alfonso of Castille, 9 Felipe II, 16 Civil War, 17 Franco

NATURE PHOTOGRAPHERS LTD 68 Sierra de Guadarrama (Paul Sterry), 70 Lesser Kestrel (Kevin Carlson), 71 Green Winged Orchid (Paul Sterry), 72 Crested Lark (Dr M R Hill)

The remaining pictures are held in the Association's own library (AA PHOTO LIBRARY) with contributions from:

Jerry Edmanson, Philip Enticknap, Tony Oliver